The Broken CEO

How To Be The Leader You Always Wanted To Be

CHRIS PEARSE

Copyright © 2020 Chris Pearse

All rights reserved.

ISBN: 978 17 04928 32 6

DEDICATION

This book is dedicated to you, the leader,
who seeks true leadership through self-leadership,
and self-leadership through self-awareness.

Know Thyself, and to thine own Self be true.

ACKNOWLEDGEMENTS

I acknowledge with sincere thanks the many CEOs, directors and senior managers who have allowed me to practise and hone my craft with them. A big thank you also to Michael Hastings for his insightful foreword. Credit and thanks to Richard Pearse for designing the artwork and Nicole Tickle for proof reading. A special mention to Dean Orgill, Guy Perricone and Chris Lamb, who provided invaluable feedback on the draft manuscript. A big woof to Coco and Poppy who forced me to take them for walks when it was the least wanted, but most needed distraction. And a debt of gratitude goes to Julie-Anne, Richard, James and Lucy, without whom this book may never have been written. All unattributed quotes are courtesy of William Shakespeare - or whoever really wrote those wonderful plays.

CONTENTS

FOREWORD		1
INTRODUCTION		3
PART 1	**The Broken Leader**	7
	The Unhappy Leader	12
	Stress and Strain	18
	Conflict and Dysfunction	23
	Ill-Health and Dis-Ease	29
	Mediocrity and Failure	34
PART 2	**Me, Myself and I**	41
	It's All in the Mind	47
	Conscious Rest	55
	Living On Purpose	65
	Balance, Equanimity and Resilience	78
	Imagination	87
PART 3	**You, Us and Them**	99
	Good Behaviour	102
	Influence	111
	Give Up and Let Go	119
	Say No… Often	124
	Speaking and Listening	132

PART 4	**The Complete Leader**	**139**
	Delegating Trust	143
	Not Telling but Coaching	150
	Chaos and Stasis	158
	Values vs Value	167
	Upside Down Leadership	173
CONCLUSION		**181**
APPENDICES		**185**
	I Meditation	186
	II Development Programmes	192
	III Resources	193
ABOUT THE AUTHOR		**196**

FOREWORD

When we think 'CEO' we rarely link the word *broken* in the same phrase. Maybe *successful* or *dynamic* or *powerful* or *strategic* or even 'the turn-around CEO' or 'the fresh start CEO' but rarely broken!!! We assume that the thought of a Broken CEO is one who isn't performing to Board expectations, and so is driving the business way adrift of shareholder gains and way beyond the public duties of responsible public leadership. A Broken CEO would be ousted, gone, finished, done over! Not so. A broken CEO can be like any of us – full of flaws and beholden to fears and fretting about performance - knowing full well that the conversation or situation was just not right, let alone clearly not good... let alone the baying pressure of your people. Demand after demand.

Meanwhile, the CEO strides onward through the business looking smart and leading the executive with constant confidence... but the inner world is far from content or purposeful. It's a huge dilemma. As companies have gone from local entities to global power centres, and as regulatory duties and public stakeholder expectations have become accountable entities rather than just wishes and hopes, the CEO must too become all confident and all capable. If only that were easy!

If this book helps some to look for greater team capacity to share the burden, and guides others to truly believe in finding daily peace in order to be more effective to lead, and even causes some to honestly assess whether the stress is a price worth paying, then I'm grateful that Chris Pearse has found the guiding tools we all need to speak truth to ourselves and to build a better world for others, because we are better people both inside and outside.

Lord Dr Hastings of Scarisbrick CBE

INTRODUCTION

What if your whole experience of leadership could be transformed from one of frustration, conflict and stress into freedom, purpose and fulfilment?

If you already feel completely free, purposeful and fulfilled, then put this book down and get yourself a cup of coffee before your flight is called. But the chances are that you don't *quite* feel that way. You have done at times, which is why you know exactly what I'm referring to - the memory persists. But those times are either past or all too fleeting. Today you have the worries of the world on your shoulders.

What keeps you going? Is it the income, a need to succeed, loyalty to your friends and colleagues - or just an acceptance that this is how things are, this is as good as it gets?

The good news is: it doesn't have to be like this. I know this not just from my own experience, but that of the many CEOs, directors and senior managers whom I have helped transform their experience of leadership from one of resignation to exuberance.

The great news is: it starts and ends with you. You don't need to change who you are, you just need to become more familiar with what I call your *inner dynamics* - your inner worlds of thinking and feeling. When you get intimate with them, everything changes.

Knowing yourself better leads you to understand why you cannot change some things no matter how hard you try. It leads you to focus on the things you can change instead. The intelligence behind this approach is that those things you can't change are better off left alone.

Or as a New York hotel concierge once told me:

"Sir, I can get you anything you want - and anything I can't get, you don't want"

Although this book's title appears to aim it at CEOs, the subtitle suggests a wider constituency: Leaders. In fact, the book pertains to anyone and everyone, simply because - without wanting to sound trite - we're all leaders. Whether we're leading a FSTE100 global behemoth, a smaller organisation, a division, or leading a team - the same insights apply. At home, as parents, we have to take the lead on occasion - and even a hermit has a life to lead. Leadership, or more properly self-leadership, is a critical aspect of all human life.

Introduction

This book is all about the dynamics of leadership - the thinking, feelings, beliefs, aspirations, behaviours and mindsets, which create our experience of organisations. It does not specifically address the mechanics of leadership, which I would define as the practical, managerial, strategic, operational, financial and commercial dimensions of running an organisation. These are beyond the scope of this book.

Advocates of evidence-based best practice, derived from scientifically rigorous research, will be disappointed. All I concern myself with is what works for me and my clients and our shared experience of leadership. I would urge you to prioritise what resonates with you above all else. For a gong to resonate, it needs to be struck with a mallet. You are the gong, this book is a mallet.

The Broken CEO does not purport to give you all the answers. In fact it quite possibly raises more questions than it does answer them. This is deliberate. Although answers are needed in the world of work and leadership, we often do ourselves a disservice by seizing on answers without due consideration to the questions they emerge from. Questions open up the mind to possibilities - answers shut it down. *I don't know* is a truly powerful state of mind, which will engage curiosity and invite knowledge and wisdom to flow. *I know* excludes all alternatives. One of the many quotes, questionably attributed to Albert Einstein, says:

"If I had only one hour to save the world, I would spend fifty-five minutes defining the problem, and only five minutes finding the solution."

Whether or not he said it, it emphasises how any judgement, decision or answer can only be as good as the reflection on which it is based - an essential premise of this book.

For that reason, however intimately aware you may be of how dysfunctional our leadership of organisations, people and ourselves can become, I would recommend that you read all four parts of the book in sequence to get the most from it. The suggestions for change in the remaining three parts make most sense from the perspective developed earlier.

PART 1

THE BROKEN LEADER

What exactly is a broken CEO and why use such strong imagery? According to one source, broken means: separated by force into parts, not integral or entire. It's a powerful picture, but before we explore it further, I want to invite you to make this personal.

This book isn't about other people - this is about you and me. It's about my experience of leadership and leaders and about your resonance with what I'm saying - not a dry, intellectual resonance, but a visceral feeling. Because, as we'll discover, much of leadership is about feeling, rather than reason.

So how can a CEO - or any human for that matter - be broken? How can they be not whole or complete? The answer seems to be: very easily. And it's reflected in some of the common language, which we use without a second thought:

> I felt all over the place
> He was beside himself
> She was in pieces
> I was a shadow of my former self
> It was a shattering experience

Each of these imply a disconnection between ourself and… ourself! And in that seeming paradox, lies some good news:

You are not broken!

It may indeed feel like it at times but, as we'll see, it's all a bit of an illusion, simply because your self and my self are indivisible. With due regard to those suffering psychoses, which are beyond the scope of this book, experiencing more than one self is not the norm.

Of course our personalities can change with time and experience and our mood may swing between extremes. But the innermost self, which experiences existence - the *I am* that precedes words such as cold, happy or frustrated - seems to be the one constant throughout our lives.

You can break everything around it - as I have done - but it remains the still, observing presence, unchanged and unchallenged, and certainly unbroken.

Awareness of this self, which lies at the centre of each one of us, is a key - perhaps *the* key element of this book. It leads us to the inevitable conclusion that, however broken, fractured, dysfunctional, inept, unhappy, unfulfilled, miserable, depressed and ineffective we may feel, in reality that self is whole, complete and experiences the entirety of our existence, untouched by it.

Which begs the question:

How do we connect with and experience that completeness?

Answers follow once we've explored exactly what the Broken CEO experiences and feels in the day-to-day business of leading an organisation.

The feeling of not being whole or complete - of being broken - can be experienced in many different ways, at different levels of our being. In Part 1 of this book we explore this sense of being broken as it manifests physically, emotionally, relationally and in terms of leadership.

The chances are you've experienced at least one of these. Some leaders experience many of them. The feelings can be very intense causing some to change their lives completely; some, even to end it all. Caught early, these feelings signpost the need to evolve. Ignored, they do not go away, they simply become more insistent until we take heed.

A common mistake that many of us make is to attempt to change the situations, or the people around us who don't conform with our ideals. We react to others' behaviour with irritation, ignorant of the fact that the feelings are wholly self-generated. Unless the other person is aware of this mechanism and consciously avoids it, they also get irritated. Now we have two for the price of one!

As we'll see, when the focus of change is on your inner world of thinking and feeling, rather than the outer world you find yourself in, everything changes for the better. It's so much easier to shift your thinking than someone else's.

This book is a manual for inner change: a means of taking action - inner action - when our outer world seems to be at odds with us. Our human system gives us everything we need to take this action. But first we need to recognise - to feel - the need for change. The system gives us that too - in the form of feeling not right, out of sorts, unhappy with ourselves and our experience. Let's see how that unhappiness manifests.

The Unhappy Leader

Thou seest we are not all alone unhappy

The net result of feeling broken is a feeling of unhappiness or discontent. A knowing that things could be better and a desire to feel good - to feel happy, fulfilled and at peace with ourselves and the world around us.

Many CEOs do not feel happy. I have met plenty who admit that they are a long way from feeling how they would like to feel, doing the job they do. I have met even more who betray their unhappiness through their behaviour, whilst being unable or unwilling to admit it to themselves, or to share it with anyone else. The drive and ambition that get CEOs and directors into leadership roles can be the same factors that hold their development back.

You will have experienced a degree of unhappiness yourself - as I have - which can manifest as one or more of a number of archetypal personas. Here are a few of the more familiar ones:

The Worrier

Thinking about what could go wrong is your speciality. You can create countless negative scenarios and keep them turning over in your imagination until they seem the most likely outcome. This skill helps you to defer decisions until the last possible moment and then obsess over the all-too-likely calamitous results.

Sometimes you're right, which vindicates your approach, but often you're not. You justify your anxiety as planning for the worst case, but it saps your strength and you just can't get any respite from the worry and doubt.

The Imposter

In spite of considerable success and achievement, you just know that one day, you'll get found out - that someone will see through the veneer of your leader's title and find… nothing. You don't really have the experience, or the credentials - let alone the confidence and know-how - to do this job.

God knows how you got into this position - you wanted it at the time, but you really don't merit it, and soon the game will be up. What will you do then?

The Victim

Ever since you took on this role, you've been at the mercy of those around you. If it wasn't for them (and some of the adverse situations you've had to endure) things would have turned out very differently. You'd like to make radical changes to your team but you're aware that the board might resist. Besides, recruitment is a minefield these days so you're probably better off with the people you have - better the devil you know...

There's nothing much you can do about it now - the die has been cast - you might as well do what you can and struggle on.

The Casualty

You're giving everything to the organisation. You work long hours, you miss children's birthdays, your anniversaries - you even missed Christmas once. Weekends at home are a luxury. Sure, you're well paid, but is it worth it?

You're overweight, out of shape and frequently breathless. Headaches are daily, you're sleep-deprived and suffer from acute indigestion and backache. The doctor says your blood pressure and cholesterol make a heart attack likely unless you make some radical lifestyle changes. You will, but not now.

The Blamer

You are surrounded by incompetence. Your team seems incapable of taking instruction even though you go to extreme lengths to tell them what to do, when to do it and how, leaving no room for misunderstanding.

People continue to mess up even though you keep reminding them, in no uncertain terms, of the consequences. You work on the basis that your people need to be kept under pressure to get much out of them, and that if you let up for a moment, they'll take advantage. It's the only approach that works.

The Pauper

Money doesn't grow on trees and there's never enough to go around. The business needs more cash to thrive, and so do you. If you can cut expenses back enough, you might be able to break even and start to pay off some of the debt, which is beginning to weigh heavily on you and the business.

There is so much that you want to do but funds won't allow. It'll all have to wait until the situation turns around and cash starts to flow. In the meantime you prune everything to the absolute minimum to hopefully see out another few months.

The Miserable Millionaire

The business makes plenty of money but it doesn't give you the security you yearn for. You need more, just in case something goes wrong and you lose what you have.

Oddly you seemed happier when you had less money, as you had less to lose. Now the stress of making sure you hang on to your wealth, in such uncertain times, is taking its toll on your health, your relationships and your life.

The Misfit

Your heart is not in this anymore. It's not really what you wanted when you took the job but the salary made it attractive at the time. Every morning you have to haul yourself out of bed with the prospect of another long, onerous day looming large.

When you reflect on it - which you try to avoid - you know the world wouldn't miss what you're doing. And nor would you. It wouldn't miss the business either but at least it keeps a few people in work who, incidentally, seem to hate it too. Where is the meaning?

The People Pleaser

You go out of your way to treat others with respect and avoid conflict when you can. After all, teams work better when everyone is getting on with each other. But if you're honest with yourself, you realise that you've been avoiding conflict because you want to be liked - you hate the idea of colleagues thinking ill of you.

Pleasing people has made a rod for your own back because now you are surrounded by people who can't handle conflict - perhaps they can't handle the truth? You don't really know as you've managed to circumvent the robust, authentic conversations, which get under that veneer of niceness.

•

These nine examples of unhappy CEOs are by no means exhaustive, but they cover many of the thoughts and feelings that clients have expressed to me. The chances are good that you will have experienced at least one of them - directly or indirectly - at some time in your career.

The details are, however, a sideshow for now. The net result of these dysfunctional states is a feeling of unhappiness - a longing for the fulfilment, serenity and contentment that we know is in reach, if only we could access them and live in them.

And it doesn't stop there. Unhappiness is pernicious - it seeps through the best defences and impacts your team, your decision-making and performance, before eventually undermining relationships with friends, family and loved ones. Ultimately it challenges health and wellbeing, emotional, mental and physical.

In the following chapters we'll take a closer look at the causes of unhappiness and how, if left unchallenged, they can lead you to that state of feeling broken.

•

Roundup

- Success is a feeling, not a figure
- Good egos and bad egos are still egos
- Don't blame the situation, or the people
- You are both cause and effect
- You are not broken

STRESS AND STRAIN

The quality of mercy is not strain'd

Get a piece of raw spaghetti and hold it at both ends, between your fingers. Now flex it gently so it bends slightly away from you. Release the bending force so it returns to being straight again. You can do this any number of times and the piece of spaghetti will return to its original shape, showing no memory of what you did to it - that's called *elasticity*. Play with it.

If you break it, get another piece and start again.

Disclaimer: I have not tried this with every brand or variety of spaghetti and can't guarantee the same results with each!

Now bend it gently away from you until it snaps. Often it will break into several pieces due to the propagation of shock waves. However it breaks, the change is permanent.

Imagine doing the same with a straightened-out paperclip. The wire will behave in the same way at first - returning to normal after bending. But go beyond a certain point and instead of snapping, the paper clip will bend permanently - it will have a memory of what you did to it. This is called *plasticity*.

In both cases, bending them beyond a certain point results in a permanent change - the difference being that you can bend the paperclip back into shape - more or less. The spaghetti is beyond repair.

You may remember from school Physics that the force you apply to either the paperclip or the spaghetti is called *stress*. The change in shape (the amount it bends) is called *strain*.

Both these terms are used rather more loosely when it comes to describing how we feel if things aren't going our way. Our vernacular uses many stress and strain metaphors:

> I cannot stress enough how important this is.
>
> The strain is beginning to show.
>
> You must be under a lot of stress.

These metaphors can shed some light on human behaviour when we explore the physics behind them:

Because stress is an external force and strain is the reaction to it, what we experience as an unpleasant feeling is not stress at all, it's strain. That is why you and I could be subjected to the same situation and react quite differently to it.

If our bank accounts were emptied overnight and all our assets confiscated, that would create a degree of stress for most of us. For some, the internal response (the strain) would be such as to spur us into action to recuperate our loss. But for others, it could trigger a severe emotional reaction resulting in a total inability to take any effective action at all.

The same stress applied to the length of spaghetti and the paperclip will have a completely different effect in terms of the strain they both experience. The paperclip might flex a little and return to normal once the stress has been removed. The spaghetti could snap, never to be the same again.

So what are you made of? Are you made of steel or are you more like a length of pasta? Before you answer this rhetorical question, consider one of Aesop's Fables - The Oak and the Reeds:

> An Oak that grew on the bank of a river was uprooted by a severe gale of wind, and thrown across the stream. It fell among some Reeds growing by the water, and said to them, "How is it that you, who are so frail and slender, have managed to weather the storm, whereas I, with all my strength, have been torn up by the roots and hurled into the river?" "You were stubborn," came the reply, "and fought against the storm, which proved stronger than you: but we bow and yield to every breeze, and thus the gale passed harmlessly over our heads."

Clearly there is a third type of material that undergoes more strain than metal or pasta for the same stress, but which never breaks and always returns to its original form. It has a degree of elasticity that allows it to return to shape regardless of most circumstances. Another word for this is *resilience* - the ability to bounce back emotionally - which we will be exploring further on.

Although stress and strain are not the same, as I hope to have demonstrated above, I'll be following the convention of using *stress* to denote both, unless otherwise stated.

Executive stress - the stress of leading an organisation or a team - is often experienced as a disparity between what you, as the leader have, and what you want. The nature of the difference is unique to the individual but generally revolves around performance, relationships and behaviour. In other words:

- The organisation is not meeting its objectives
- Relationships between any two stakeholders is sub-optimal
- The behaviour of one or more people is below the standard required

Very often it's all three.

Identifying these failings in any organisation is straightforward - many overflow with them. The resolutions can be more elusive, particularly when our attention is consumed by the effects of the issues, rather than the causes.

•

Roundup

- Stress is the difference between what you have and what you want

- Stress is a human construct

- Are you spaghetti, paper clip or reed?

- Performance, behaviour and relationships appear to cause executive stress

- Resilience is the ability to bounce back from stress

CONFLICT AND DYSFUNCTION

There are few die well that die in a battle.

If stress is the gap between what we want and what we have, conflict arises from the difference between how others behave and how we would have them behave.

Perhaps the biggest mistake we make, when it comes to addressing conflict, is believing what we see. An easy assumption to make is that conflict is overt - if two colleagues are not getting on, the result will be fairly obvious to all. Both parties will eventually make their feelings felt and some kind of eruption will take place making it clear to everyone that the relationship is dysfunctional and requires intervention.

In practice a very different sequence of events plays out where the fight or flight options are replaced with a freeze response. Let's take an example:

Susie is the Marketing Director of a global tech company. She needs to oversee a digital marketing strategy for the launch of a new audio product. She seeks help from Tom, the Engineering Director. Susie knows nothing about audio design. Tom knows little about marketing. Tom's focus is the performance of the product of which he is understandably proud. Susie's interest is in what the market wants.

Susie seems to discount the technological achievements - just as many users might. Tom, feels that the huge technical efforts and breakthroughs, which he orchestrated during the product's development, are being taken completely for granted. He feels the irritation as a vague clenching in his torso but pays little attention to it. Whenever he has to communicate with Susie on the strategy, it gets the better of him and he becomes abrupt and unhelpful. She, frustrated and annoyed by Tom's apparent emotional immaturity, disengages and relies instead on resources other than Tom's knowledge, even though there is no one better placed to help her.

Whenever they're together in executive board meetings, they sit apart and pretend the other is not present. No one else is aware of the breakdown in their relationship. The conflict is covert - the dysfunction is hidden behind a mask of indifference.

Because both parties are keen not to externalise their true feelings, this is a freeze response. Fight or flight necessitate giving the game away to all concerned.

The conflict is marked by a gulf between the behaviour Tom and Susie want from each other, and the reality. But it goes deeper than that. They want each other to think and feel differently. Tom wants Susie to have more respect for the technology. Susie wants Tom to show empathy with the users.

Short term, the freeze response appears to work for both of them. The feelings of frustration, irritation and anger seem preferable to whatever emotions might emerge if either of them broke cover and went public.

Some months later, the product launches but the impact falls far below expectation. A post-mortem by the executive board reveals serious shortcomings, omissions and untruths in the messaging. In essence, the marketing material promotes an idealised version of the product - a marketing aspiration as opposed to a technical reality, exactly mirroring the root of the conflict between Susie and Tom.

Now the nature of the dysfunctional relationship between the two surfaces for all to witness. Tom and Susie engage in open conflict (they both choose to fight), blaming each other and attempting to exonerate themselves. The ensuing battle follows a well-trod path on which Tom's inability to defend his position causes him to take stress-related leave whilst Susie, unable to recover from the loss of face, moves on to another company.

The emotional toll, which the drama takes on its protagonists, is heavy. Tom never forgets the humiliation he felt in front of his colleagues when the truth came out, nor the fear at the potential consequences. It still makes his stomach knot to recall it, in spite of all the techniques he learnt from his therapist during his leave.

Susie will never forgive him, and her perception of all engineers is tainted by the experience. She bridles whenever she has to collaborate with a technologist, instinctively distrusting and discounting them, male and female alike. Her career, if not ruined, was severely curtailed, by taking a huge drop in pay and status.

Mark, the CEO, also took a big hit. He nearly lost shareholder confidence as a result of the failure. He was lucky to remain in post. He now manages his team with maximum scrutiny and a minimum of trust. It's not the place he once knew and loved, and he is not the same person, as his wife and children will attest.

One of the most powerful factors to drive conflict is *point of view* as this oriental fable illustrates:

> Three blind men come across an elephant. The first man happens upon its leg, and concludes it's a tree. The second man bumps into its trunk, and concludes it's a snake. The last blind man feels its tail, and concludes it's a broom.

Neither one will understand why the others perceive so differently unless they are prepared to forsake their own limited points of view. That is a big ask for many. But it is quite conceivable that the three of them could work together to reach a common understanding, given a genuine desire to comprehend the differences.

Sometimes it is simply not possible for all parties to share an understanding. Not only will there be different points of view to contend with, but blind spots too. With a blind spot what you see clearly, I will be quite unaware of and never able to see like you.

All of us have blind spots in our ocular field of vision. This natural blind spot is due to a lack of receptors where the optic nerve and blood vessels leave the eye. But you only know about it when something that you could see before, disappears from view. The reason we don't see a black hole in our field of vision is because the brain fills it in with something plausible.

Fortunately, because our physical point of view is changing constantly, whatever finds itself in our blind spot, doesn't stay there very long. Pretty quickly, we will have seen everything in the field of view - all we have to do is move our eyes.

Regrettably this doesn't happen when it comes to mental perception. All too often, our point of view becomes so fixed that we never perceive whatever lies in our blind spots. In the mental realm we can have as many blind spots as we wish and our very clever brains will fill them in with something that makes sense and hides whatever truth may be hiding in it.

The only way to avoid becoming severely misled by our own blind spots is to recognise that we have them, even though we may have no idea what they are, or how they affect our perception. This is an aspect of self-awareness that is critical to leadership. Conflicts like the one described above can be transformed by just one person willing to change their point of view, even if only temporarily.

Nota Bene: by self-awareness I am referring to the fullest possible experience of being alive, not simply a definition of our personality type provided by one of the many psychometric tests available today - the latter being a very small and limited aspect of our human existence

•

Roundup

- Much conflict is covert
- Fight or Flight has a third option: Freeze
- Our blind spots get filled in so we can't see them
- Blind spots and assumptions trigger conflict
- What I am blind to, you may see clearly

Ill-Health and Dis-Ease

*Diseases desperate grown,
by desperate appliance are relieved, or not at all*

A premise of this book is that the unhappiness we feel is an outcome, not of the circumstances that we encounter, but our response to them. The way we bend, snap or bounce back is determined by our inner world, not our outer one.

When the stress (or more precisely, the strain) goes beyond a certain point, psychological and physical symptoms emerge, as the following quotes testify:

"Studies in both animals and people show pretty clearly that stress can affect how the brain functions. Health problems linked to stress include cognitive problems and a higher risk for Alzheimer's disease and dementia. There is evidence that chronic (persistent) stress may actually rewire your brain." says Dr. Kerry Ressler, professor of psychiatry at Harvard Medical School.

"Stress affects not only memory and many other brain functions, like mood and anxiety, but also promotes inflammation, which adversely affects heart health." says Jill Goldstein, another professor of psychiatry and medicine at Harvard Medical School.

"When under stress, cells of the immune system are unable to respond to hormonal control, and consequently, produce levels of inflammation that promote disease. Because inflammation plays a role in many diseases such as cardiovascular, asthma and autoimmune disorders, this model suggests why stress impacts them as well." according to Sheldon Cohen, professor of psychology at Carnegie Mellon University.

Many of the problems we encounter, which appear to be the cause of unhappiness, can often be traced back to our thinking, and the ideas that we believe - our beliefs.

The quotes strongly suggest a causal link between stress and disease. Somewhat tellingly, the word disease originally meant without ease.

Not so long ago, some ailments, which have no apparent physical cause, were being written off as *psychosomatic* or "all in the mind". ME or myalgic encephalomyelitis, is a case in point. Also known as CFS (chronic fatigue syndrome), ME presents as a debilitating condition described by the NHS as: "extreme physical and mental tiredness (fatigue) that doesn't go away with rest or sleep." Today, treatment plans include CBT (cognitive behavioural therapy) which is a non-physical intervention focussed entirely on changing the way the patient thinks.

Fortunately, today we are seeing a growing awareness that non-physical health issues are as real and significant as their physical counterparts - just that the non-physical causes demand intervention in our emotional and psychological worlds.

Antonio Horta-Osorio (group chief executive of Lloyds Banking Group) gave us a stark reminder of how bad things can get. In 2011, within months of starting the top job, he spent nine days at the Priory clinic to prevent a nervous breakdown. His insomnia had reached a tipping point that he said was affecting his abilities.

"It almost broke me," he said to The Times. "I thought I was Superman. I felt I could do everything. Before this, I had thought that the less sleep and the more work, the better. It showed me I was not Superman. And I became a better person, more patient, more understanding and more considerate. It was humbling, but you learn."

"I was not used to asking for a lot of advice or showing a lot of [emotion] because I'd been a CEO since the age of 29 and it is a very lonely job – people require leadership, even in moments of adversity and difficulty," he said. "To go from there to this humble experience and learning to 'share' with someone else, yes, it required some learning, I admit."

Horta-Osorio was perhaps lucky to have avoided the physical impact of this kind of extreme stress. Others have not been so fortunate.

In 2015, Oscar Munoz, the CEO of United Airlines, had a major heart-attack. Munoz was on a 90-day listening tour of the US to meet irate employees and customers. He was flying economy on scheduled flights and getting little sleep. In a sense, he was flying around the country to get criticised and blamed - the sole target for collective anger and hatred.

Munoz was well aware of the impact of lifestyle on health. He was a vegan at the time, who stayed fit through cycling, tennis and golf. His apparent good health did not seem able to protect him from his job and its impact on his physical wellbeing. Munoz returned to work the following year, the recipient of a new heart.

Sometimes the ultimate sacrifice to wellbeing is made with no physical illness at all. In 2013 Pierre Wauthier, 53, CFO at Zurich Insurance Group, took his own life and left a suicide note. The note suggested that his chairman had placed him under intolerable pressure. Although the allegations were denied, the chairman quit shortly afterwards.

It would appear that whenever our emotional balance is compromised, there is an opposing force, which is trying to re-establish equilibrium. So it would seem that certain external situations cause some of us to undergo a stress reaction which, if neglected long-term, can cause physical illness.

There are some ideas which, when they take root, create not only pathological emotions, but eventually physical disturbances, including disease.

Catching the imbalance early avoids our natures upping the ante until we either take action voluntarily, or are compelled to do so.

•

Roundup

- Psychological stress can lead to physical symptoms
- "All in the mind" makes it more real, not less
- More work does not make for better outcomes
- Your mind and body will do whatever it takes to make you listen
- Sometimes the damage is irreparable

Mediocrity and Failure

Be great in act, as you have been in thought;

The ultimate expression of leadership is often considered to be excellence and success - particularly financial success. The antitheses to these benchmarks are mediocrity and failure. Yet curiously, boardrooms can tolerate, even reward activity when performance is evidently below acceptable standards.

Carillion, the construction and outsourcing company, provided an example of abject failure in 2018 when it underwent one of the largest ever trading liquidations in the UK. A parliamentary committee called out the "recklessness, hubris and greed" of its directors who continued to enjoy ever-larger remuneration packages against a background of mounting debt and pension deficit. Carillion actively exploited suppliers whilst their accountants, KPMG, vouched for figures that "misrepresented the reality of the business" according to MPs.

It's hard to imagine the atmosphere in a boardroom complicit in such a monumental failure of leadership. There must have been more than a whiff of deliberate neglect and conspiracy to deceive, which would have perplexed anyone with even a shred of moral rectitude.

In contrast, failure is becoming the new success, as we are exhorted to "fail fast, fail often" by entrepreneurs and innovation experts, frequently citing Thomas Edison as an exemplar of this philosophy.

Of course the difference between a Carillion failure and an Edison failure lies in the intent behind the activity, and its scope. Because the intentions were fundamentally different, so were the two ultimate outcomes: the electric light bulb; a broken company.

As we'll explore later on, the intention behind activity represents the cause behind the effect - the thought behind the action. To engineer a successful outcome, we need to shine our light back up the chain of cause and effect to our inner world of thinking and feeling, exposing the thoughts, ideas and beliefs that lie above and below the radar - not just those we know about, but those that remain beyond the limits of our ordinary perception.

Mediocrity is the state of being in the middle. It's neither one thing nor the other. The word used not to have the negative meaning associated with it today, but even so, there are some states where being in the middle is not a desirable position.

Being halfway up a mountain is best avoided as anything other than a transitory phase. You need to get to the top, or return to basecamp, not remain neither up nor down like the Grand Old Duke of York. Similarly in terms of your position in the market, there has to be something about you that is different, which sets you apart and forms your unique selling proposition, without which getting noticed becomes a challenge. When leadership delivers mediocrity across the board, failure is the inevitable outcome.

The UK retail sector is currently awash with well-known companies going into administration. Yet, notwithstanding intense online competition, some of those at both extremes of the market - well away from the mediocre middle - continue not just to prosper but to thrive: Harvey Nichols Group in 2018 revealed its EBITDA up 102%; In 2019, Primark half-year profits surged 25%.

Excellence in some areas can more than compensate for deficiency in others. For several years, Easyjet opened its doors to a warts-and-all documentary team that delighted in showing the general public everything to dislike about flying with a budget carrier in the 21st century. Yet, in spite of this apparently detrimental exposure, passenger numbers grew and in 2018 the shares peaked at nearly seven times their 2000 price. Easyjet must have been doing something right.

Ed is the founder and CEO of a tech company. He devised an elegant solution to the problem of maintaining continuity of the electricity supply to rural and remote locations. Exploiting a number of different leading-edge technologies and combining them in an ingenious way, he came to market before anyone else could. Ed's creativity presented both a benefit and a challenge to his company. He quickly recruited some good people around him but always seemed to have more insight than they did. Similarly, he saw opportunities for different applications of his technology and wanted to approach all the markets that they could open up. When new technology arrived, he was an early adopter, integrating them into his expanding product portfolio.

All of this would have been fine for a £100M company - regrettably, Ed's wasn't even £100K. The upshot of Ed's energy, creativity and vision was a range of products, addressing several different markets. Yet neither Ed nor his team had a track record in any market other than one, and only one working prototype existed.

Ed had seen a range of mountains in front of him and had decided to climb every one of them. He was now committed to them all, being at best halfway up only one, and still at basecamp on all the others. He was spread way too thin and so was his team. His self-belief in the face of adversity created a micromanager out of him that alienated his people, and isolated him. It also burnt cash at an alarming rate.

The business managed to attract an investor with deep pockets and a penchant for technology, but no real idea of its commercial application. The influx of cash did what money often does - it amplifies whatever is going on and makes it bigger. In Ed's case, it facilitated more products, more applications and more markets. It failed to bring any one initiative to fruition. Conflict escalated, people left and the company is now dormant.

As a brilliant engineer with a flair for disruptive innovation, Ed could inspire others with his vision. But he had an overriding belief in his view of the world, to the exclusion of anyone else's, and a misplaced confidence in making unaided decisions across the whole spectrum of business activity; blindspots aplenty.

The investor fixated on Ed's brilliance, perceiving the lack of funds as the fundamental barrier to success - a problem he could overcome by writing a cheque. But the real problem was Ed's lack of self-awareness and understanding of the inner dynamics that were relentlessly driving him to mediocrity in execution, and ultimate failure.

Ed's primary mistake was to believe that projecting confidence would compensate for not feeling it. Sometimes Hamlet's advice to 'assume a virtue if you have it not' can shift the way you feel about yourself - like adjusting your posture, head up, shoulders back. But Ed had become reliant on the veneer of confidence to permanently compensate for feelings to the contrary. The result was a personality that not everyone appreciated.

•

Roundup

- Mediocrity is being in the middle - sometimes a good place to be, sometimes not

- You may not be great at much, but you need to excel at delivering your value

- Failure is simply just another outcome, which we can learn from

- Reward failure and you'll get more
- Failure is the result of thinking that needs correction

The Broken CEO

PART 2

ME, MYSELF AND I

Just consider for a moment who you are.

Your name will perhaps come to mind, followed by an awareness of your body - two arms, two legs, a means of digesting food, breathing air, converting energy, fighting infection.

Then, of course, your ability to speak, listen and think is a vital part of who you are - and all the other stuff that goes on from the neck up.

Fundamental too is what goes on below the waist, without which none of us would be here.

And then there are your feelings which we'll be exploring in more detail later.

Your subconscious mind is also a key player in who you are, though just how much remains a mystery until it becomes conscious.

Yet all these aspects of me, myself and I are accrued over time. Our physical aspects grow, develop and wane over the course of our lives. Our mental aspects change according to our environment and experiences.

Your body's cells are anything from a few years to a few days old - the renewal process is unrelenting from birth to death. None of us physically is who we were last week, let alone last year.

Our mental worlds are even more dynamic, with thoughts able to change in an instant and our moods fluctuating rather like the weather. Personality, beliefs and assumptions shift in response to our situation.

Everything is changeable. Or is it?

Here's a thought exercise that you can run right now:

Become aware of You. Not your body, personality, name, mood or thoughts... just You. Imagine peeling back all those physical, mental and emotional accumulations so that only one thing remains: You. Just get a hint of it, if you can.

Now cast your mind back to that same sense of You when you were a child. Remember it's not how you thought and behaved as a child, which hopefully will be very different, it's how you were. Children are much better at doing this kind of thing than we are, so you should be able to tap into a memory of that experience of just being.

What you may realise is that the sense of being when you were a child and that same sense now, have not changed. The sense of I am is just the same now as it always has been - and will not change while you are alive on this earth.

The only things that have changed are all the accumulations which we describe ourselves by:

I am hungry - I am tired - I am excited - I am a CEO - I am overweight - I am successful...

The core sense of being, which lies behind all identity, thinking and feeling, remains the same.

Have you ever woken from a deep sleep at a complete loss as to where you are, what time it is, what day and year it is, your past and your future, even who you are in terms of your age, your name, your purpose? It's not an uncommon experience. If you are not familiar with it, all that you are left with is a sense of being - I am. Then, very quickly, all the missing information gets recalled as you return to a normal sense of who you are, your past and your future. Being precedes thinking.

This experience directly contradicts René Descartes' famous dictum: *I think therefore I am*, suggesting the reverse is closer to the truth.

It all starts with *I am* - everything else unfolds from that. And the mistake we make is to conflate the I am with all the adjectives and nouns we put after it. Our attention is absorbed by the title, the job, the stress, the promotion, the beliefs, the family, the holiday - all the trappings of modern life. There's nothing wrong with any of these (though I'm sure you'd rather avoid the stress) other than the belief that they form our true identity. When you invest your attention in a belief, you believe it. *Believe* has the same roots as *love* - you invest your love in it and it becomes dear to you; it becomes a part of you. This is often easier to see in others than yourself.

You may know someone whose lack of self-esteem flies in the face of their obvious talents and experience. Yet, time and again, their feelings of unworthiness and incompetence, which have no real substance, hold sway over them and hold them back from fulfilling potential. Their beliefs are so tightly held that, regardless of how absurd they are, no one can disabuse them.

Now, chances are, as a fully paid-up member of the human race, you are likely to be in the same predicament as your friend above. The nature of the beliefs that you hold about the world and, in particular yourself, may be quite different, but some of those will be having a regressive effect on your development. Me too.

What I'm suggesting is that anything variable, anything that you can add to yourself, take away or modify, isn't, in reality, you. It's an accretion, an artefact - rather like a suit of clothes or even a mask similar to those used in Greek dramas. Just because it's held as an idea in mind doesn't make it less real. But when you really believe it, it can be hard to remove - and that's regardless of whether you like the idea or not.

So not only do we have a mismatch between who we are (the being part) and who we think we are (the thinking part), there's also a difference between who we think we are and who others think we are. Herein lie the seeds of discord and conflict.

In Part 2 we explore the approaches we can take to loosen the hold that our thinking has on us so that we remain more closely in touch with who we really are, rather than accepting and believing the ideas in which we have invested - ideas that supplant our being with thinking.

Becoming more familiar with who we really are, behind all the changeable thoughts, ideas and beliefs, puts us in greater contact with ourselves. It promotes self-awareness, the essential precursor to leadership. In fact it facilitates self-leadership, without which no true leadership can take place. Self-leadership - the ability to lead oneself, the ability to lead one's life - has to be mastered to some degree before we can hope to lead anyone else, let alone an organisation.

And as I hope to show, leading an organisation is no more than an expression of self-leadership through a heightened sense of self-awareness - knowing who we are.

IT'S ALL IN THE MIND

*The fool doth think he is wise,
but the wise man knows himself to be a fool.*

What is the mind? We use it constantly, we experience it without any let up, we employ it from birth to death. And yet many of us have little clue as to what it really is.

Neuroscience is making great strides in uncovering the electrical, chemical and structural secrets of the human brain. Our minds seem to be located within this vast neural complex; any disturbance to the physical structure of our brain can have major repercussions on our psychological integrity, suggesting a strong link between mind and brain.

Yet the experience of your mind is not limited to the space between your ears. You can quite easily transport yourself to a memory of an Italian holiday whilst remaining firmly on your sofa. With a well-developed imagination you can create a life on Mars, at least temporarily.

Looking out of the window, you see a cat stalking a bird. All the neural activity enabling your awareness of that event is taking place exclusively within your head - and yet the cat and the bird are clearly some metres away from you. The cat crouches and gets ready to pounce. You feel a hint of adrenaline. Just for a fleeting moment you identify either with the hunter or hunted. You are not in your head anymore - to a degree, you *are* the cat or the bird.

The difference between the mind we experience - the *subjective mind* - and the brain that facilitates it - the *objective brain* - is key to discovering who you are. Notwithstanding the remarkable progress, which is being made through researching the secrets of the brain, it is the mind that we experience. We have complete, unrestricted, 24/7 access to our subjective mind and its workings. Whereas access to the objective brain and its functionings is restricted to a few elite scientists, who are still scratching the surface of what is really going on amongst those 100 billion neurons.

Because of the greater intimacy we have with our mind over our brain, I'll be confining my observations to the subjective mind, with all due respect to, and recognition of the discoveries being made in the field of neuroscience.

One advantage we have in doing so is that we can draw on bodies of knowledge developed over millennia of experience, which humanity has used to observe its own subjective minds.

One such body of knowledge stems from the yogic tradition of ancient India which offers a remarkably simple and practical model of the human mind that we can put to good use.

But first a few words about the language in which this knowledge was recorded: Sanskrit. Sanskrit is the language of ancient India which has found its way into many modern European languages. In English the words: same, name, naval and nose derive from the Sanskrit words: sama, nama, nava, nasa, respectively. More significantly, Sanskrit has an abundance of different words for concepts, which may be represented by only one word in English. For example, the word love has scores of different words in Sanskrit; the word imagination has at least 4 equivalent words in Sanskrit.

All these different words are not synonyms for the same concept. Just as Icelandic has many different words for snow, each word means something different and represents a subtlety of understanding and a detailed knowledge that requires several words in modern English.

The large number of words, which Sanskrit has at its disposal to describe the human system, suggests a fluency and familiarity - a wisdom - lacking in those traditions with a more restricted vocabulary.

Let's briefly explore some yogic thinking around the human mind and how it works.

The yogic model of the mind comprises four parts:

> Intellect, Memory, Identity, Intelligence.

Intellect is that part of mind that has been revered in the West for several centuries. It is the faculty that is trained in schools and universities often to the exclusion of other dimensions of mind. It is sometimes likened to a sharp knife, or the sword wielded by Lady Justice atop London's Old

Bailey criminal court. The intellect analyses, dissects, discriminates and passes judgement on whatever is presented to it. The intellect is located in the brain.

The intellect needs memory to operate. Our assessment of a new situation can only take place in comparison to what we have already experienced in the past, held in memory. But memory is not limited to the brain. Nearly all of our 30 trillion cells contains DNA which is an ancestral memory. A bruise is a memory of an impact. Tiredness is a memory of exertion.

The identity is more than just ego - it gives you your sense of who you are. It is the identity that defines the scope of the intellect and often uses the intellect to defend itself. After all, the intellect is a sword. So, however sharp the intellect may be, its scope is qualified by the identity.

Finally, intelligence is a far greater concept in yogic science than intellect. It is intelligence that allows you to eat an apple and for that apple to become you, rather than for you to become an apple. It is intelligence that operates your physical body from moment to moment. If you try to control breathing with your intellect, you won't last long. Intelligence requires no memory and has no central location. It is simply there, maintaining life as we know it.

Yogic science says that intelligence connects to the basis of creation within you. It connects you with your consciousness. We get a hint of this when we are 'in the flow' or deeply connected to an activity. All we have to do is sit back and watch the intelligence do its thing.

When you observe yourself from this yogic point of view, several things become clearer:

Firstly, the intellect is a very limited aspect of who we are. It is simply a means of mentally dissecting whatever we put in front of it. The identity - who you think you are - determines how the intellect is used. So if a sharp intellect is in the hands of poorly developed identity, chaos can ensue.

Secondly, the individual can wreak as much havoc on themselves, with their intellect, as on others. This is the basis of poor self-esteem, self-criticism and low self-confidence. Self-harm of this order can also set the scene for anxiety, depression and other psychological disorders.

Thirdly, the intellect protects the identity. When you become a supporter of your local football team, you start to dislike other teams. If you are a pacifist, you'll see the military in a bad light. When you buy a new car, it'll be better than any other.

Finally, intellect is not intelligence, which is a faculty that transcends identity. If you have any doubts that intelligence is non-personal, ask yourself if you could grow your hair, heal a broken bone or pump your heart if that intelligence was suspended.

You may have noticed that so far in this chapter, there's been no mention of feeling or emotion. Significantly, yogic science discriminates less between thought and feeling than modern Western thinking. This is because thought and feeling are essentially intertwined. They are the two faces of the same coin. It is unusual - perhaps impossible - to have a thought without a feeling and vice versa.

One yogic commentator suggests that thoughts are 'dry' and feelings are 'juicy' but they are the same thing. Thoughts are quick to summon and dismiss - emotions and feelings linger for longer. Just because your partner is now your ex-partner due to infidelity, doesn't mean you won't feel heartbroken for some time to come. Rationally, the relationship is over - you have separated and there is no overlap in your lives. Emotionally, the feelings stay with you, and a feeling akin to bereavement can last for much longer than you might wish.

In contrast to this yogic perspective, recent neurological research suggests that maybe thinking and feeling are distinct. In the early 1990s, the neuroscientist, Antonio Damasio, used a study of brain lesions to demonstrate how impairing the emotions can degrade decision-making capabilities. Removing brain tumours left some patients with their ability to reason fully in tact but without any facility to feel.

Damasio tells the story of one patient who retained his highly developed intellect after the operation, and could continue to present the logical implications of various complex scenarios. But he was rendered incapable of making the simplest of choices such as selecting a restaurant or booking his next appointment.

Whether thoughts and feelings are inextricably intertwined as yogic wisdom asserts, or they are discrete phenomena as neuroscience suggests, the fact remains that feelings are central to our decision-making process.

Those of us, frequently men, who defend our decision-making as purely logical and immune to feeling and emotion, are quite simply wrong. The faculty of feeling drives us in one direction or another in a way that reason can't do. The word emotion comes from the latin *emovere* meaning to move out, a metaphor for a decision made.

That is not, for a moment, to suggest that we abandon reason - but that reason, analysis and rationale inform the way we feel. We need to do our intellectual homework prior to making any decision, but then to embrace our feelings knowing that they and they alone will guide us at the moment of choice.

So how do these insights play out into the way we lead ourselves, our lives and our people?

Firstly, we need to maintain a heightened sense of feeling. We need to admit the whole spectrum of feeling and emotion to our awareness, initially discounting nothing. We know that the feelings are ours, but they are not us. So we can observe them, feel them, with a degree of objectivity and curiosity.

Secondly, we need to be able to suspend our faculty of judgement - our intellect - at will. To use a popular metaphor, we need to sit on the fence. Stretching the metaphor somewhat, it is indeed true that fence-sitting can get quite uncomfortable after a while, but it does allow us to see what lies on both sides. As soon as we jump off, we lose the bigger picture.

Thirdly, we need to create a space in which the decision can emerge. That space is silent. In music the absence of a note is referred to as a rest. It is only in that state of rest that we can perceive what may be quite subtle. Agitation is the enemy of intelligent decisions.

•

Roundup

- Life is entirely experienced in our minds
- The subjective mind is not the objective brain
- Thought and feeling are two sides of the same coin
- All decisions are determined by how you feel
- Our feelings are ours but they are not us

CONSCIOUS REST

The rest is silence

Work-Life Balance has become a popular focus for anyone concerned with maintaining mental and physical health at work. But there is a problem at the heart of the concept: work *is* life. So the implication of balancing your work and life is that they are mutually exclusive: when you're alive, you're not at work; when you're at work, you're not alive. This is clearly absurd. I want to be just as alive when I'm working as when I'm not. I imagine you to be the same.

This false dichotomy between work and life rather crassly suggests that we are expected to feel lifeless at work - that work is hostile to life and neither life-affirming, inspiring nor energising. Of course this is how work has felt to many of us at times, possibly all the time for some. Good leadership, particularly good self-leadership, leads us towards integrating work and life, making work a meaningful expression of our lives - enabling us not just to survive, but to thrive.

So the real balance to be had is not between work and life, but between work and rest. Work and rest are the opposing states that need to be in harmony with each other. Neither too much, nor too little of either. The quality of each is interdependent: good rest means good work; good work means good rest.

Most likely you will be acquainted with work in its many forms: hard physical labour; late nights spent meeting crucial deadlines; hours of concentration mastering a brief; chairing of critical, high-stakes meetings; being in the flow of doing what you love. But fewer of us are so familiar with rest in its various forms, many of us engaging in activities which we believe to be restful but which, in reality, are anything but.

Let's take a closer look at what we mean by rest.

Rest has three common meanings:

1. Repose or cessation of action

2. What remains or is left over

3. A support for something

As the counterpoint to activity, rest does all three of these: it provides respite from work; it is what remains when work ceases; and, critically, it supports work.

Before we examine rest in more detail, let's explore some analogies for rest.

Firstly, sound in the form of music. In music, the counterpoint to sound is silence. There is either one or the other, never both simultaneously. So if sound corresponds to activity, the silence corresponds to rest. Significantly, the musical notation for silence is called a rest.

Now a musical novice might easily be forgiven for thinking that the music is in the notes that are played - the sounds that are made. Yet, one of the greatest musicians, and composers, ever to have lived, Mozart, would disagree.

He said:

The music is not in the notes, but in the silence between.

What did he mean by this? Well at a practical level, it's pretty clear that you can't make decent music without some space between the sounds. Admittedly, there are some genres of music that allow very little space between sounds - some almost none. But there has to be some variation in the musical dynamic, some nod to the underlying silence, to qualify as music, and to maintain interest from the listener.

At a more subtle level, the silence supports the sound - all music rests on silence - it starts and ends in silence. What remains - the rest - once the music is over, is silence. The silence is ever-present - the music is transitory and ephemeral. Unlike other forms of art, music cannot exist outside of the present moment, the immediate now. Perhaps it is the contrast between the eternal silence and the fleeting sounds, which gives music its appeal.

Another analogy of rest is the white space on the piece of paper (or screen), which you are reading right now. In this case, the black type equates to activity, the white space to rest. To demonstrate the interplay between space and type, try to read the following paragraph:

whenyouremoveasmuchwhitespaceaspossiblefromthewritt
enwordtheamountofinformationthatyoucanstoreonthepage
increasesbutitdoessoattheexpenseoflegibilitytheresultanttex
tbecomesdifficulttoreadthemeaningbecomesobscuredbythe
highratiooftypetowhitespace

Here is the same paragraph with more space and punctuation:

> When you remove as much white space as possible from the written word, the amount of information that you can store on the page increases, but it does so at the expense of legibility. The resultant text becomes difficult to read. The meaning becomes obscured by the high ratio of type to white space.

The balance between space and type is critical to the ease with which we assimilate the message. One can imagine how a piece of the most sublime, inspirational poetry could be rendered irritating and meaningless through ignorance of the fundamental balance between black type and white space. Perhaps the same applies to work and rest.

Just as silence supports sound and the white sheet of paper supports the text, so does rest support work.

So the relationships between sound and silence, white space and black type, are obviously critical. Thanks to the creativity of musicians and the skill of typographers, we don't need to worry too much about them. We know what music appeals and we discount what doesn't. If a page is badly laid out, perhaps strewn with unwanted adverts, we may ignore it regardless of the information it holds.

However, when it comes to the balance between work and rest, which we choose to observe in our daily lives, we have far more discretion.

What forms does rest take in the life of a leader?

Jo leaves work around 6.30 pm, sometimes later. She slides into the leather upholstery of her 4x4 and switches the radio on. Her 40 minute drive home is time she cherishes. She likes driving, particularly this car, and she can switch off, alternating her attention between listening to the music and reflecting on her day.

Arriving home, she's greeted by her dogs and plays with them. She takes a quick shower, pours a stiff drink and puts her feet up in front of the TV. She watches the news until she hears her partner arrive home from the gym. They chat about each other's work, prepare dinner and wash it down with a bottle of good wine.

Next they watch a Netflix drama, with laptops and phones providing intermittent distraction. Jo goes downstairs to their home office to call the US for an update. At roughly 11pm they both go to bed, tying up any loose ends by phone. No time to read a book tonight, lights off around midnight. They rise at 6am and both head for different airports. The cycle continues.

Other than occasional distractions and interruptions, that scenario includes a number of activities associated with rest. Playing with dogs is known to reduce blood pressure.

Showers, alcohol and TV all assist with relaxing and winding down. And swapping between work emails and Facebook is perhaps less demanding than being at work.

Then there is sleep. Sleep remains one of the great mysteries of human existence. Where are we when we're asleep? Where is our consciousness? Sleep has become the focus of much interest from neuroscientists, none of which seem to yet have definitive answers to these questions. I would argue that we already know all about the most important aspects of sleep. Firstly, that it naturally synchronises with the hours of darkness. Secondly, that we need a certain quantum of sleep to maintain wellbeing.

Our bodies and minds are very efficient at telling us when we haven't had the amount of sleep that we need. We ignore the signs at our peril. But rather than slavishly following the received wisdom on how much sleep you need, I advocate sensing how sleep makes you feel, and adjusting accordingly. There are many of us who would suffer through sticking rigidly to the 8 hour rule.

So far we've considered sleep, alcohol, dogs, TV, showering and putting your feet up as facilitating rest. There are undoubtedly many more, which we could add to this list. Now I hope to convince you that fundamentally none of these represent real rest at all - even sleep - as they all miss a crucial element, without which there can be no true rest, however much sleep you get.

Every activity in Jo's evening routine encourages physical or mental activity. Nothing wrong with it, but it's not rest. Rest is inactivity - mental and physical. Sleep is, of course, largely inactive, at least physically, but who knows what mental activity is taking place. Many of us have experienced waking up exhausted after a night of emotional turmoil, however still our bodies have been.

The missing element for most of us is *conscious* rest - full awareness with no activity other than that required to keep us alive. Jo's evening represents a typical period of relaxation for many leaders and yet each activity she engages in requires mental exertion. Even blobbing out on the sofa leaves the mind idling on anything that takes its fancy, flitting from TV to Instagram, to reflections on the day past and aspirations for tomorrow.

What is lacking is the ability to disengage from the activity of the mind and simply observe with no agenda and no motive. This is a very simple process. Unfortunately, as simple as it is, it seems so difficult for many of us, thanks to the layers of habit and resistance, which get in the way:

As we discovered in Part 1, our identities are closely bound to our intellects, so closely that many of us believe that we *are* our minds - particularly the discursive faculty of mind that presents us with an infinite flow of ideas, perspectives, judgements, opinions and beliefs. This is the Monkey Mind of Buddhism, the inner voice, judging others and ourselves, never settled or content, feeding from a constant stream of external data: news, views, adverts, social media, gossip and information.

Having allowed this one aspect to dominate for so long, we consider it the norm. Yet some of us will do almost anything to get away from it through a spectrum of displacement activities, which include food, sex, alcohol and the pursuit of power, wealth and success. All of these work to blot out the inner cacophony, but only temporarily. Unless the individual aspires to connect with aspects of being beyond the mind, addiction to some form of distraction is a very real hazard.

So how do we do this? How do we get respite from the relentless mental activity, in which we find ourselves immersed?

The first thing to understand is that you will not stop the mind doing what it does. Would you want to stop your heart, your liver or your lungs from their activity? As soon as you tell the mind not to do something it will go and do just that. Tell yourself now not to imagine a giant blue rabbit nibbling your toes and see what happens.

So rest from mental activity does not mean making the mind still. It just means observing the activity, rather than *being* the activity. As soon as you put some distance between you and your thinking, the activity starts to abate, but not through any action on your part, purely through disengagement.

The mind is like a glass of water with earth in it. If you shake the glass, the earth gets disturbed and the water becomes opaque - unclear. Leave the glass alone for a few minutes and the earth settles - the water becomes clear.

In other words, we give the mind the rest it needs - the rest we need - simply by leaving it alone for a while. We remove stimulation, we keep the body still and we give ourselves a very simple focus of attention. This is the essence of meditation, the single most potent aid to self-development that I know of.

All my clients establish a simple, secular meditation practice early on in the programme and report profound shifts in the way they respond to the people and situations around them.

The reason it works seems to be the way in which it interrupts our habitual understanding of the world and ourselves, progressively allowing new perspectives to infuse. As yogic wisdom puts it: before you can know what you are, you have to discover what you are not.

Meditation is the purest form of conscious rest available to us. If you aspire to the highest expression of leadership and self-leadership, meditation is a non-negotiable foundation to your work. Or as we might say today: it's a no-brainer - metaphorically and practically.

To establish your own practice, turn to the Meditation appendix and follow the instructions. If you have tried meditation in the past and 'failed', you have simply allowed your lower mind to call the shots. There is no failure in meditation. You either practice or you don't. Even the apparent quality of the meditation is unimportant - that's just another judgement of something your intellect doesn't understand. Invoke the goddess of victory and just do it.

·

Roundup

- Work-Life balance is a false dichotomy

- Work-Rest balance is critical

- Rest is to work what paper is to writing and what silence is to music

- We need conscious rest - many of us get none

- Meditation is the foundation of good leadership

LIVING ON PURPOSE

> *So may a thousand actions, once afoot end in one purpose,*
> *and be all well borne.*

What is your purpose?

Ask yourself now.

It's a blunt question. It almost asks you to justify your existence, suggesting that without a purpose you have no value.

You may feel a little better as you start to answer with phrases like:

>   Look after my family
>   Lead my organisation
>   Create wealth
>   Make a difference

You may see your purpose less in terms of a lifetime's activity but more as a series of objectives:

>   Get promoted
>   Holiday in the Maldives
>   Donate to charity
>   Make a million

However you express them, they are all finite in scope, being unfulfilled one moment and complete the next. In looking after your family, each relative will progress from one stage to another, requiring a completely different approach. When children leave home, the empty nest can present the parents with a need to significantly realign their purpose.

Your worldly purpose, whatever it is, unfolds as a series of discrete steps, actions or objectives, which are aspirational one minute and complete the next.

These mechanics of purpose pose a bit of a problem for some. Take professional sports people, particularly olympic competitors. They spend perhaps four years of their lives preparing for an event which may last less than ten seconds. They win or they lose. Silver doesn't really cut it for the ultra competitive.

Yet paradoxically, winning can present the competitor with an even bigger problem than losing. Once the celebrations have subsided and the winner is back home with their medal, basking in the glory of success, the question that will ultimately emerge is: What next?

The loser, on the other hand, may have another opportunity to prove themselves in the future, and can immediately start planning their revival and their journey to victory.

Double Olympic gold medal winner, Victoria Pendleton, suggests it's almost easier to come second because you have something to aim for when you finish. When you win, you suddenly feel lost. What she describes is the immediate loss of purpose as soon as it is achieved.

A very similar phenomenon exists in leadership. The term Summit Syndrome (coined by George D. Parsons and Richard T. Pascale) describes the feeling of emptiness, which can immediately follow the attainment of a hard-won goal - a success - particularly in terms of career progression, promotion and getting to the top of the ladder.

In work, it is all too easy to divert one's attention from the loss of purpose through attainment of a goal, by immediately targeting another. The problem is, this strategy is not sustainable - sooner or later we have to come to terms with the fact that the achievements themselves do not satisfy - they seem to lack meaning. Achievement without meaning is rather like the icing without the cake. The pen without paper.

The need for a continual stream of achievement - winning - can become addictive. But, as with all addiction, the gratification is short-lived and the need for meaning will not relent.

Purpose, when properly identified and wholeheartedly felt, provides the foundation for achievement with meaning. But what does it actually mean?

The word purpose derives from the Old French verb *porposer* - to put forth. So the emphasis is on what you put out into the world, not so much what you achieve, or get back. This is an important clue. It is a practical reality that we have much greater control and influence over what we put out, than what we get back in terms of results, achievements etc.

On that basis alone, our purpose needs to focus on our activity and our output, over and above our results and achievements; what we put out, not what we get back. John F. Kennedy alluded to this when he famously proclaimed:

> "Ask not what your country can do for you – ask what you can do for your country."

So what is your purpose now?

Are you any clearer as to what it is?

If not, do not be anxious. Not having a clear and well-defined purpose is a common syndrome, which many leaders suffer. We'll be exploring ways of clarifying your purpose shortly. But first let's listen to what some great leaders have to say on the subject of purpose:

The C13th Sufi mystic, Rumi, suggests we all have an innate purpose, which needs to be found, not chosen:

> "Everyone has been made for some particular work, and the desire for that work has been put in every heart."

Leonardo da Vinci was reputed to have said:

> "Make your work to be in keeping with your purpose"

inviting us to work *on purpose*. Ask yourself now if your work is on purpose.

Finally, a quote from Henry Ford sounds a warning to us all:

"There is no failure except failure to serve one's purpose."

Having worked with many clients on their purpose, I would suggest that following a clear purpose which resonates with what we love, which allows our gifts to flow out into the world, and which delivers tangible value to others, is one of the cornerstones of self-leadership and of leading others through example.

How do you get clarity of purpose? As with much self-discovery, revealing the truth is often a case of discarding untruth. Frequently, we can invest our lives in purposes that turn out to be digressions. Saul of Tarsus famously changed his purpose (and his name, to Paul) from collecting taxes to saving souls, on the road to Damascus. The clarity was so intense it blinded him for 3 days. The many examples of people leaving highly-paid, banking and finance jobs - to connect with something deeper within - is evidence of the power this inner calling can exert.

Some never quite seem to connect with a deeper purpose, dying in their prime, but buried in their dotage. Bronnie Ware, is an Australian nurse who spent several years working in palliative care, caring for patients in the last 12 weeks of their lives. She wrote a book called The Top Five Regrets of the Dying, revealing their final insights:

1. I wish I'd had the courage to live a life true to myself, not the life others expected of me.

2. I wish I hadn't worked so hard.

3. I wish I'd had the courage to express my feelings.

4. I wish I had stayed in touch with my friends.

5. I wish that I had let myself be happier.

These observations emerge when everything but the final breath is removed from the individual. At the end of life you can start to shed all the stuff you think you need to live. There is no further need for ambition, aspiration, entertainment or gratification. Any kind of pretence, insincerity, bluster and ego need energy you don't have, and has no point anymore. All that is left is a memory of the past to reflect on. Many report a lucidity and clarity of mind at this stage of their lives which facilitate the kind of insights that Bronnie Ware recorded.

The No.1 regret is Purpose. At its heart is a great sadness: living the life others expected of you. Even sadder when you realise that, in reality you may have lived the life you *thought* others expected of you - did you ever stop to ask them?

Self-leadership invites you to work on purpose - that you not only achieve, but that you do so with meaning, a meaning that fulfils.

So how do we identify our purpose if it's not already crystal-clear? If you have any doubts as to what your purpose may be, I will now describe a very simple process, which you can use to get more clarity on this critical question.

But first we need the right perspective on the issue. Not all of us - however off-purpose we may feel - are going to have a Damascene conversion. Any expectation of one simply serves as a distraction. Just an incremental shift, however small, is enough to begin the process which will unfold in perhaps a very unpredictable way. As is often the case, we need to concern ourselves with the what, not the how.

This process of clarifying purpose can unfold over the course of a week. On each day find 5 minutes when you will be undisturbed and able to sit comfortably with your eyes closed. First thing in the morning is a good time, before the children wake up. Ask yourself these questions 1 day at a time and don't jump ahead:

Day 1: When you are physically idle (not concerned with doing anything) what do you tend to think about? Do you daydream about things - if so, what?

Day 2: What do you tend to do when time and space allow? What activities do you gravitate towards, other than relaxing?

Day 3: What used to excite you as a child? Think back to the activities that you loved when you were young.

Day 4: Do you have any unfulfilled ambitions? Things that you want to achieve, which you've had to neglect because of practical considerations?

Day 5: Think back over your life and identify those things that you've been particularly good at, even though they may seem unimportant or of little value.

Day 6: Imagine that all the responsibilities that seem to restrict your time suddenly disappear. What would you do with your new-found time and freedom?

Day 7: Imagine that you have a very large bank balance - far, far more than you need to live as you do, for the rest of your life. How would you use it?

If over the course of the week you had a blinding epiphany and have already left for the Himalayas to join a monastery, all well and good. Many of us though, have obligations, which are very much a part of our purpose, and radical change is neither helpful nor desirable. For others a step change is needed. Only you will know what it is that you seek, once you can see a little beyond the layers of thinking that can hold you back.

The purpose of the exercise above is simply to delve beyond the habitual ideas and beliefs, with which we can easily justify our circumstances - one of the most powerful being around money and finances. Our attitudes towards money can easily define the life we live. The words "I can't afford to" can set the limits on who we are and what we become. It is a sentence every bit as powerful as that passed by a high court judge.

Our understanding of money can be quite confused:

> Money is the root of all evil

> Money makes the world go round

These two common adages illustrate how attitudes to money can cover a wide spectrum. In fact, the first saying is a misquote of a bible verse which states:

> The *love* of money is the root of all evil.

But that does not alter the fact that many use it and believe it.

Money doesn't grow on trees is another favourite, even though paper money clearly does exactly that. Even with the proliferation of digital money, the process of Quantitative Easing - a strategy employed by central banks to increase the money supply - is arguably a means of creating money out of nothing.

Whatever your attitude to money, be prepared to let it go at least for a moment, particularly on the seventh day of the exercise, just to see what lies behind it and how it may be holding you back.

Julia ran an arts academy with a global profile. She had made a significant impact through building a great team around her, raising the academy's standing, and overseeing a huge infrastructure project, which transformed the organisation's ability to deliver on its remit. She had been a highly successful CEO in every respect. But she wasn't happy. Something was missing. She and I worked on clarifying her purpose and she eventually realised that her future lay in directing theatre productions, something she had done in the past and loved.

Julia understood this. It wasn't a revelation, rather it was a confirmation of what she already knew but hadn't acted upon for several reasons: the time wasn't right; she wanted to finish on a high and wasn't quite there yet; she didn't relish a drop in salary; she didn't want to be seen to be walking away when a difficult issue was raising its head. All perfectly viable reasons, but all in opposition to what she really needed to be working on purpose.

Her foray into leading an academy had been on purpose at the time, but now she was being called to a different way of delivering her value - and for less money.

Job done? Not quite. Despite her decision to move on, the months passed and she got embroiled in various issues around relationships and personalities at work, which made her life very difficult indeed. She started to wonder if she was trying to leave just to escape an unpleasant situation - quitting and fleeing. The question of purpose had once more become muddied.

Although Julia had seemingly made a decision to leave, she had acted on it in a cursory, non-committal way - hedging her bets. What was needed was definitive action, a courageous step into the unknown. Not a few tentative, exploratory conversations but a clear statement of intent. After I spoke with her, she made contact with several head-hunters and influential, industry figures, and within weeks had landed a job, which now allows her to work on purpose.

Her previous objections to moving no longer hold water. Her remuneration package although lower than it was, is not an issue. On reflection she values her many achievements prior to leaving, not just the loose ends she left behind, which pale into insignificance by comparison. And she realises that what other people think of why, when and how she left, is simply none of her business. There will always be detractors and supporters of anyone in a leadership role, and the job is never finished.

The kind of purpose we've considered so far is our purpose in the world - how we bring our particular skills and insights to bear on our environment. How we make a difference. It's often characterised by some future goal, which we are looking to fulfil - the direction we're going in. Eckhart Tolle (author of The Power of Now) calls this our *outer purpose*. It's all about how we manifest our thinking into action. As we've seen, clear thinking is central to working on purpose.

But there is another purpose in addition to this, which Tolle labels our *inner purpose*. This is not concerned with future goals, but with our presence in the here and now. Our inner purpose is about connecting with our selves, which can only ever take place in the now. It's remaining aware of the *I am*, over and above what, who, where, why and how *I am*. As soon as you move into qualifications of your *I am* you move out of the present moment into a past that is dead or a future that is yet to exist. That is not to say that you need to spend your life floating 6 inches off the ground, in a lotus position, eyes closed, humming Om. It does require us to realise that the only real satisfaction and fulfilment comes from the present, never from what has been, or what is yet to come. The olympic athletes who thrive emotionally are those who derive their purpose from every moment of life, in or out of training, winning or losing. The medal is a bauble, the podium ceremony a sideshow - every moment has purpose.

Having considered inner and outer purpose, we need to realise how our outer purpose can only be fulfilled via inner purpose. Another way of expressing that is to say that we can only get to fulfil a future goal through a step taken now - right now. This present step is all that exists - we never experience the future as the future, only as the now. So from that point of view alone, all thoughts beyond the present are a dilution of reality and purpose.

In this inner purpose lies the true meaning of mindfulness, which is simply a state of being present to your self and your environment. Being present is being now. You cannot be yesterday or tomorrow - only now.

This inner purpose is common to us all - our only choice is whether we embrace it or not. Our outer purpose is a function of our circumstance and the gifts and aspirations we find within ourselves - all of which can evolve over the course of a life.

The purpose of leadership, in my view, is to empower others to take full responsibility for themselves - and in this process of growth and evolution, to lead others to their self-leadership.

What's your purpose?

•

Roundup

- Purpose is what you *put out*

- Your purpose needs to be aligned with your work for you to feel fulfilled

- When you are focussed on purpose, you don't need to worry about what you get back

- You have an inner and outer purpose

- Your inner purpose is to connect with life in the moment

Balance, Equanimity and Resilience

> *If the balance of our lives had not one scale of reason to poise another of sensuality, the blood and baseness of our natures would conduct us to most prepost'rous conclusions.*

Balance is generally accepted as being a good state to be in. If we refer to someone as unbalanced, that's a pretty severe indictment of their ability to function as a human being. It's a given that we hope to maintain balance, independently of circumstance, as far as we can.

Let's consider the physics of balance to understand it a little better. Physical balance is essential to remain upright and be able to walk around. We balance our centre of gravity over the pivot of our feet on the floor. Too much weight on one side or the other, forward or backward, needs correction to prevent falling over. We have wonderfully sensitive organs of balance located in our ears, which allow us to stand and walk upright with our centre of gravity above the balancing point - a fundamentally unstable setup. Try standing on one leg with your eyes closed to verify this.

We balance our intake of food with the amount of physical exercise we do in order to maintain optimal weight and waistline. If the balance between calories ingested and calories expended gets out of kilter, so does our shape and ultimately our health.

As Iago, in Othello suggests in the quote at the head of this chapter, we also balance our primal urges with reason, to avoid unpleasant consequences.

So balance applies across the spectrum of our physical, mental and emotional worlds. To create balance, we need to deal with two opposing qualities. Those qualities may be identical on either side of the pivot, as in the example of balancing our posture by the distribution of weight. Or they may be intrinsically opposed such as the centripetal, and centrifugal forces, which maintain the Moon in its orbit. Either way, they balance out.

How then do we know when we are in balance? Emotional balance is a feeling not dissimilar to that of physical balance. When we're off balance on skis or a bicycle, we feel it and take immediate, corrective action to prevent a fall. Imbalance in our emotional world is also experienced as a feeling, one that we are all familiar with. Emotionally, we have a little longer to adjust than we do skiing, but the principle is the same.

In order to understand the means by which we can all take the corrective action to establish and maintain emotional balance, let's explore the very simple relationship between thought and feeling.

Thoughts can be triggered by an internal reflection (a childhood memory for example) or by an external event such as unexpected news. In practice there is no difference between the two - both stimulate a thought in mind. The thought almost immediately leads to a feeling. The quality of the feeling will be a function of many things, not just the event. It will include your mood, your state of mind, memories, habits and experiences. This is why different people react to the same event in a variety of ways.

The feeling, or emotion, will drive a reaction - remember that emotions move things, they have (e)motive power. You will then decide whether or not to externalise the reaction.

So the pattern of events is very simple: an event triggers thought; the thought leads to feeling; the feeling drives a reaction. Whether the event or the reaction are internal or external changes nothing, as it is the feeling that we experience.

A friend of mine described how he was sitting in a London café with an Italian friend, visiting for the first time. In Italy, it is not unusual to look at a stranger and maintain eye contact for rather longer than a Londoner would - it shows interest and regard. In London it is considered intrusive and rude. Oblivious to this code, the Italian stared at a local in the way that you might in Rome, to suddenly find himself on the floor with a sore chin.

In this example both the stimulus and the reaction were external, the latter clearly being a function of personal and cultural memory. The Londoner's thought that the stare was hostile triggered emotions strong enough to override any sense of reason, balance or fear of consequence. A harsh lesson hopefully well learnt, at least by the Italian.

Given the intention behind the Italian's stare, the local's reaction was, by any standard, out of balance. Give yourself a few moments now to recall situations in which your reaction to an event was unbalanced. The examples need not include any physical violence!

Note also that although thinking can change in a second, feeling requires much longer. This is why you can retract things you have said, but not always the feelings they evoke. Or as Chinese folk legend, Monkey, put it:

> "A word that has left the mouth cannot be overtaken by a six-horse chariot."

Having established the sequence of events linking thought, feeling and reaction, let's now consider how we can intervene in the chain of cause and effect to mitigate and balance the results.

Firstly, we need to accept that we have little or no control over the external events that come into our lives - the rich tapestry, the vicissitudes, the slings and arrows will continue to present us with a myriad of experiences. Our only choice is how we respond.

Secondly, we need to sharpen our focus on this internal thinking/feeling mechanism. To observe it means disengaging and distancing ourselves from it so that we can see it in operation. With attention, you will be able to perceive the space between the thought and the resultant feeling. This is a space of choice and free will - do we grant full rein to whatever emotion arises, based on the past, or do we allow intelligence into the space?

The intelligent option has nothing to do with intellect, which can only operate on past data. It is best described as a calm, collected knowing, present only in the here and now. We have all experienced it and we all have access to it.

The nature and operation of this intelligence is beyond both my powers of description and the scope of this book, but it lies at the centre of who we are, our self-awareness and our capacity to lead ourselves and others.

Deliberately interrupting our habitual, reactive behaviour patterns in this way is the key to establishing and maintaining emotional balance. Even counting to ten can be a highly effective means of avoiding unwanted emotion.

The knee-jerk, habit-driven, negative behaviour is a reaction to events. We are seeking to replace it with an intelligent, chosen *response*. Responding rather than reacting is a life-changing behavioural shift, which benefits everyone involved. It is what the world increasingly needs and it is is very, very simple. But simple does not always mean easy.

What we're up against in this mission to change our inner dynamics, is layer upon layer of habit, belief, paradigm, mindset and memory. We may have practised reactive behaviour since childhood, so change may not be instant. We may have been schooled by our parents as Philip Larkin describes in his irreverent poem *This Be The Verse*. Many cultural influences, from advertising to politics, encourage us to react rather than respond. Almost certainly, we have invested a chunk of our identity in some of these ideas, to the point where they are a part of who we think we are. Any challenge to them is perceived as an existential threat.

In the classic Hindu epic, The Geeta, Lord Krishna exhorts Prince Arjuna to slay his enemies in battle. The problem is that the opposing army comprises many of Arjuna's revered friends, relatives and teachers. Arjuna doesn't want to fight them. Metaphorically, we face the same predicament as Arjuna in rejecting ideas, views and opinions, which are very dear to us - they have been our friends, relatives and teachers. But now it is time for them to go. It is the only way to establish and maintain balance.

The ideas, which we identify with, are accretions. The yogic tradition refers to them as *samskaras* and are the direct result of our actions or *karma*. Just as every action has a reaction, so do our thoughts, words and actions result in a change to our subconscious mind.

Our error is in mistaking these accretions for who we are. When we make ideas a part of ourselves, we create an ego, which has no actual basis in reality. What's more, it is something that is very difficult - perhaps impossible - to keep in balance, simply because of the dynamic, emotive nature of the mind. We need a more reliable frame of reference.

That frame of reference is best found inside us, but not within the changeable world of our thinking and feeling mind. The best frame of reference is our natural centre of equanimity, calm and serenity - the silence behind the music, the paper behind the words, the being behind the doing. When we reference the *I am* behind our activity, we tap a still point, which provides all the intelligence we need, in the moment. An intelligence that does not rely on memory, opinion, perspective or anything subject to change.

This self-reference is the basis not only of balance, but also of resilience. Resilience is the ability to restore balance whenever it is disturbed. A resilient body allows you to recover quickly from a cold, 'flu or infection. Resilient emotions enable fast recovery from disappointment, frustration, anger, fear and loss. Resilience is the quality of bouncing back into shape after the strain of a stressful experience. The reed in Aesop's fable The Oak and the Reeds, bent with the wind, and by offering no resistance, was left intact. In the human being, resistance comes in the form of the ideas and beliefs that we gather through life, like barnacles on a boat.

The Indian mystic and author Sadhguru explains how the resilience of Indian culture has enabled it to survive centuries of occupation without the changes to its traditions, religion, philosophies and way of life that other countries have suffered. He attributes this resilience to the fact that traditionally Indians have not depended on external systems or frames of reference. He says that the country never really gets disturbed as other countries might, because for each individual: "there is an organic sense of being completely organised within (them)self... in such a way that no matter what happens, they will stay their course."

The resilient and balanced leader does not look beyond herself to self-organise, but *within* herself. There is no dependency on role models, best practice, systems and techniques. She may well adopt proven practices, and listen to experts, but her organising principle will be her self, not an imported methodology, received wisdom or a hero.

All too often modelling the behaviour of others fails simply because we are not them. We see the effects of what they do and copy the behaviour, blithely ignorant of their motives, perspectives, beliefs and experiences. Replicating their 'success' is not only impossible but, since it can only detract from our own success, wholly undesirable.

To self-reference in this way first requires self-awareness. Know Thyself was no idle decree by the Oracle at Delphi, and is as critical to our leadership now as it has ever been. And once known, Polonius' injunction also holds good:

> "This above all: to thine own self be true, And it must follow, as the night the day, Thou canst not then be false to any man."

•

Roundup

- Balance is about matching one force with another, equal and opposing

- Balance is felt - we can feel the balance and maintain it once we bypass habit and reactive behaviour

- Balance requires self-referencing, in the moment, not deferring to external frames of reference

- Referencing your inner self promotes balance and the ability to restore it when disturbed - resilience

IMAGINATION

And as imagination bodies forth. The forms of things unknown, the poet's pen. Turns them to shapes and gives to airy nothing

Imagine yourself on a desert island, palms wafting gently in the breeze. The sun warming your skin, the sea lapping near your feet. You sip an exotic cocktail and stare out at the deep blue ocean considering whether to swim before or after your massage. You get the picture…

Hopefully, without necessarily being conscious of it, your imagination was able to build this scene for you, in mind, giving some semblance of the actual experience. All that is needed are a few words to direct the creation of the imaginary experience. Note that the words triggered the process, but it was your imagination that created the result.

Some of the content may have come from memory of a physical holiday in similar circumstances, but the scope for introducing new elements is unlimited. An alien spaceship could have flown in and landed next to you at any time.

The imagination is a powerful tool. Look around now at the artefacts that surround you: tables, chairs, walls, windows, carpets, computers, lights, books. Look outside at the buildings, roads, cars and trains. Each and every one of these started life in the human imagination. They were conceived in someone's mind as a concept, which gestated in mind and eventually materialised in the physical world through human activity. Through the power of the imagination, the mind gives birth to all human creativity.

Just like any super-power, the imagination can be used for us, and against us. Many of us have slipped into habits of misusing and abusing our imagination. Recall the sequence of events that we explored in the previous chapter:

$$\text{event} \rightarrow \text{thought} \rightarrow \text{feeling} \rightarrow \text{reaction}$$

Now make your imagination responsible for creating the event, something it is perfectly capable of doing. So now the event is not taking place in the outer world but in your inner world. Thought and feeling, as usual, take place internally. In this cycle of events, the reaction is also internalised and feeds the imagination with more material:

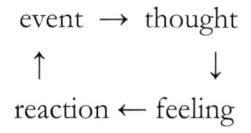

$$\begin{array}{ccc} \text{event} & \rightarrow & \text{thought} \\ \uparrow & & \downarrow \\ \text{reaction} & \leftarrow & \text{feeling} \end{array}$$

We now have a feedback loop where the output (the reaction) feeds the input. No longer is there any need for an external event, or even an externalised reaction. Everything can take place in the mind. The reaction becomes the next event. Hopefully this process is already ringing bells of familiarity. Let's illustrate this with some examples.

Driving home one evening, you remember a brief exchange with your Chair at the quarterly board meeting. She spoke over you, effectively preventing you from giving the board reasons for recently firing a member of your executive team.

At the time you were perplexed, not really understanding why she blocked you in this way. You could have insisted on being heard but you were somewhat taken aback by the intervention. Perhaps you were going to say something that the Chair didn't want the board to hear. The person concerned had been acting unprofessionally - part of the reason he had to go - but there was nothing to hide and you would never be anything less than transparent anyway. Maybe the Chair knew something you didn't, particularly since their partners know each other. You feel irritated by this possibility and can well imagine how the two of them could be communicating with each other directly, bypassing you in the process. Irritation turns to anger. How can you be expected to run a team that is being directly influenced by the Chair, without your knowledge? It's completely unacceptable. You need to address the issue immediately. But what if the Chair takes exception to your stance. You've never had a great relationship - perhaps this is just the beginning of the endgame for your job. Anger turns to fear.

In fact, the Chair had just seen a text from her husband asking her to pick up their son from school urgently. She'd felt compelled to wrap things up quickly. The next day she phones to explain, apologise and undertakes to inform the board of your reasons by email.

This process is no different from waking up in the middle of the night and seeing a ghost by the window instead of a white shirt, on a hanger, flapping in the draught.

Employing the imagination in this way is tantamount to self-harm or self-abuse. By stimulating real feelings of anger and fear through your own personal fantasy, you put your endocrine system into overdrive and become sensitised to other external stimuli. Driving home, you nearly had an accident and completely lost it with another driver.

This mechanism lies behind one of the scourges of modern life: anxiety. When we consider anxiety in this light, we can define it thus:

Anxiety is using the imagination to create what you don't want.

This begs the question: Why on earth would you use your most powerful human faculty to self-harm? It smacks of madness - of losing one's mind. Today, anxiety is listed as a clinical condition with several variants.

William Blake, the visionary romantic, said:

> "Imagination is the real and eternal world of which this vegetable universe is but a faint shadow."

What a tragedy that we can all too easily turn it against ourselves. With practice the pattern becomes established and difficult to change. Most of us will know someone who has mastered the art of anxiety and can maintain themselves in a constant state of worry. Removing one apparent cause of anxiety simply makes space for another, and the cycle continues.

With all due regard to cases of severe clinical anxiety, which are beyond the scope of this book, the kind of everyday anxiety that we witness in others and experience in ourselves can be controlled and mitigated. There are three strategies you can use without recourse to third-party intervention, medication and therapy.

The first is *distraction* which is simply, consciously diverting your attention to something more attractive than the subject of anxiety. A film, a walk in nature, dinner with friends, an hour at the gym. All of these will provide respite. Clearly though, the let-up will be temporary as this technique fails to address the root cause of the anxiety, which is your emotional reaction, not the stimulus.

The second is through *mindfulness*. The understanding of mindfulness has been diluted somewhat by the intense commercial interest that its potential as a psychological game-changer has aroused. The essence of mindfulness is being aware of the dynamics of your inner world from moment to moment. It demands you live in the now and prohibits losing yourself in vague recollections of the past or fantasies of the future. In doing so it provides you with the space and opportunity to choose how you use your mind - in particular how you respond to inner and outer stimuli. It expands the gap between thinking and feeling, giving you discretion over your response, and thus addresses the root cause of anxiety.

The third, related to mindfulness, is *meditation*. Meditation strengthens your ability to decide where your attention is placed as well as giving the mind the conscious rest that it needs. Long-term practitioners will vouch for the ability of an established, daily meditation practice to render you less susceptible to emotional disturbance, and better able to employ the imagination in a fruitful way.

Meditation and mindfulness support each other, the difference being that mindfulness can be practised in any situation. Meditation is best reserved for quiet times at the beginning and end of the day.

One of the defences that a professional worrier will cite to justify their habit is that of planning. They need to consider the worst-case scenario and be prepared for it. Planning will pre-empt any nasty surprises and leave you able to cope with undesirable outcomes. This is absolutely correct and excellent practical advice, but only needs doing once, not at every opportunity!

So far we've considered how the imagination gets easily misused by inattention and ignorance of our inner dynamics. How is the imagination best used for our own wellbeing and that of our leadership?

Being a faculty of such immense power - responsible for every pinnacle of human achievement - it should come as no surprise that the immensity of the subject of imagination precludes proper treatment in these pages.

We can, however, point to some very significant themes on the subject of imagination, which recur throughout the great teachings, philosophies and traditions of civilisations past and present.

The imagination is our tool of creation and manifestation. Anything we think, desire, say, do or build starts in the imagination.

It can work consciously: when we desire food, we make a trip to the supermarket; when we desire to build a business, we take a series of actions which are always imagined before they are executed.

It may work unconsciously: many of us report synchronicities and serendipities whereby desires are manifested through chains of cause and effect that are not clearly identifiable. The telephone rings and at the other end is the person you were just about to contact. The long-lost friend, which you haven't seen in a decade but think about frequently, sits opposite you in a café. The stranger on a plane gives you the large amount of money you desperately need for a life-saving operation, never to be seen again. If these sound far-fetched, I can vouch for their veracity.

It's easy to write off experiences that we call weird or spooky because we can't explain them in everyday terms. Yet there are many examples of physical phenomena, which can be demonstrated repeatedly and reliably, which have no comprehensible explanation. The world of Quantum Mechanics provides many of these. I am not suggesting that highly unlikely and inexplicable occurrences in our daily lives are the result of quantum physical activity, simply that the lack of explanation does not prove impossibility.

Since the dawn of history, the idea of manifestation through thought and imagination alone has been a recurring theme. Whether through the myths of sorcerers and mages like Merlin, or the modern-day positive thinking movement, the suggestion that thoughts become things is a perennial trope reflected in popular sayings such as "Be careful what you wish for."

The 2,500 year old Mundaka Upanishad is unequivocal:

> Whatever destinations and objects of pleasures the man, whose mind is free from impurities desires, he obtains those destinations and those objects of pleasures.

The only condition this ancient teaching recognises in the manifestation of whatever you want, is purity of mind.

One of the most famous creative injunctions comes from the New Testament:

> And all things, whatsoever ye shall ask in prayer, believing, ye shall receive.

The caveat here is more subtle - the process requires belief in the outcome.

Yet the common experience is far removed from these statements. Many of our deeply-held ambitions and aspirations are left frustrated and unfulfilled even after a lifetime of application. Are we misunderstanding them, or are these edicts just plain wrong?

Jumping forward to the twentieth century, Napoleon Hill, Neville Goddard and Wallace D. Wattles were all advocates of the notion that man has the capacity to think things into manifestation. They attracted large followings, possibly due to their focus on manifesting wealth.

Henry Ford betrayed a similar belief in his quote:

> "Whether you think you can or you think you can't, you're right."

Norman Vincent Peale's Positive Thinking movement followed, leading to the Law of Attraction and the Secret, all of which, at root, are based on the exact same premise, that directed thought creates our experience.

Even an arch sceptic of any kind of metaphysical activity might be hard pushed to totally refute the impact of a positive mindset. It's difficult to deny that someone with an upbeat, optimistic expectation of success is likely to outperform a depressive pessimist, at the same task.

But the power of the imagination is said by all of these sources, and many more, to go much further than just facilitating success. They are adamant that "the word is made flesh", that thoughts become things, that we have a latent power to think things into existence, through the imagination alone.

I will leave it to you to explore this philosophy further. Suffice to say that the efficacy of these systems, if true, will depend on your ability to accept the ideas behind them.

Whatever the true power of the imagination, it is the indisputable source of all achievement. Without imagination, no desire will be fulfilled, as all desires can only exist within it. On that basis alone, keeping the imagination fit and healthy would seem like a good idea. How do we do it?

Just as we strive to avoid ingesting toxins into the physical body, so we need to take the same care over what we allow to take shape in our imaginations. Here are some suggestions:

Bad news: We may need to know what's going on in the world, we don't need to dwell on it. If you are attracted to bad news and others' misfortunes, make a conscious effort to avoid it.

Gossip: Do not indulge in criticism of others who are not present.

Negativity: Refrain from involving yourself in negative conversations. Make your criticism constructive and never criticise the person, only the behaviour.

Music: Be sensitive to the effect that the music you listen to has on you, and adjust if necessary. Music has a direct and powerful emotional effect on us - choose wisely.

Social media: If your usage leaves you feeling anything but uplifted, change it. Bad news, gossip and negativity are all too often the lifeblood of online communication.

Anxiety: shift your attention from the anxiety, to observing the dynamics behind it. Remember that you are the sole arbiter of what you choose to pay attention to.

Mindfulness: practise whenever you remember. Focus on being present - there is no life elsewhere.

Meditation: establish a daily practice, for life.

Finally, if you decide to indulge in an activity that you know is not for your greater good - any of the seven deadly sins, for example - admit it, and do it well, but refuse to indulge in any guilt, self-pity or self-criticism - forgive it and move on.

•

Roundup

- The human imagination is a faculty of immense power

- We can use it to create whatever we want - what we love and what we hate - our choice

- Even at a very practical level, thoughts become things through the imagination

- Maybe the imagination can operate in hidden ways leading to serendipity and synchronicity

- We need to ensure that our imagination is maintained in the best possible health

PART 3

YOU, US AND THEM

Having explored some of the inner, personal dynamics that influence, or even determine, our behaviour, let's turn our attention to how they play out in relationship with others. However introverted, asocial and reclusive some of us may feel, much of life is lived through our relationships with others. An organisation's true value is not so much in the individuals that comprise it, as in the relationships between them. The relationships form the conduit for the flow of value between all stakeholders.

Throw a bunch of really able and willing people together for the first time and little will happen before relationships are formed.

We are highly sensitised to the dynamics of these relationships, particularly reciprocation. Most of us want a two-way flow of value. Most of us like to be treated as we treat others. Or, more accurately, as we *think* we treat others. Something in return is expected - always - even if only a feeling that we've done some good.

All these relationships are subject to the inner dynamics of Part 2. It would be tempting to assume that the challenge is to find ways of modifying our colleagues' behaviours to align with our own gold standard. Much has been written about influencing, controlling and managing others' behaviour and this is one of the biggest stumbling blocks for relationships of all sorts - romantic, family, professional and informal.

As I hope to show, the real challenge in creating valuable relationships is in managing your own behaviour first, and not taking responsibility for how others behave. Of course there are exceptions including the responsibilities parents have for children, and the need to deal with any extremes such as gross misconduct at work. But this counter-intuitive approach to relationships pays huge benefits to all concerned, regardless of individuals and context. It is another key aspect of self-leadership.

Good Behaviour

When we are sick in fortune, often the surfeit of our own behaviour, we make guilty of our disasters the sun, the moon, and the stars

The word *behave* means to contain, restrain, govern, manage or conduct. It has an emphasis on placing limits on what one does and says. Not a bad thing given what might happen if everyone on the planet gave free expression to every thought, feeling and urge they experienced, without restriction.

As a CEO, director or senior manager, your behaviour has had to be exemplary. It goes with the territory. You'd never have arrived where you are without a keen sense of how to conduct yourself in any professional situation. You present well, dress appropriately, articulate clearly and always display consideration and respect for others.

If only you could say the same of others around you. Sure, there are some great people in your organisation, but the behaviour you witness in certain individuals leaves a lot to be desired.

There's your finance director who clearly thinks he's next in line to your throne. He supports everything you say in meetings to the point of sycophancy, and reputedly quotes you in conversation at every opportunity. He also comes into your office without knocking and uses your PA as his own.

Your new sales director is getting results but he rubs everyone up the wrong way by frequently talking over them and interrupting. He has an irritating swagger about him, wears expensive suits and drives a car that you couldn't afford. He's brash, opinionated and - annoyingly - often right.

Your people director and operations director just do not get on with each other. They clearly have completely different perspectives on leadership and how to manage people. They're never going to be best buddies, but they don't even try, and you have to mediate frequently.

Every member of your executive team has foibles and characteristics, which they display through their behaviour. Some days it washes over you, but on others you really have to bite your lip.

Your external demeanour is proper, civilised, polite. But internally, you flit from mild irritation to spitting feathers. You dread meetings with your people director who will use it to vent her spleen about her operations colleague.

This disciplined behaviour goes with the role - you need to restrain and govern your instinct to tell everyone exactly what you think of them. Sometimes you fantasise over doing just that.

What choices do you have?

It's a binary one at the moment:

1. Maintain decorum and keep your feelings internalised.

or:

2. Tell everyone exactly what you think of them, and to hell with the consequences.

Your head says: "suck it up", your heart says "let them have it". In practice, of course, you don't quite achieve either. You betray your feelings through a curt reply, a passive-aggressive look, or avoidance of those that need your attention. You may fantasise over putting them in their place, even talk it through with anyone who will listen. But you never really follow through, knowing full well that indulging your emotions could bring more trouble, not less.

The persistent antipathy you feel towards some of your people can make it difficult to summon up the enthusiasm you once had for getting into work, bright and early on a Monday morning.

The stress of having to maintain a facade of composure in the face of the irritation and frustration, which threaten to overwhelm you, saps your energy and your enthusiasm.

While you see your choice as monochromatic, you are limited to two undesirable outcomes: the frustration of holding back, and the unknown of speaking your mind.

Neither is desirable, nor is either necessary.

Fortunately there is a third way which renders this choice redundant.

The third way requires us to put the insights of previous chapters into use:

Firstly we need to remind ourselves that our reaction to anyone's behaviour is exactly that: *ours*. We have complete discretion over whether we react according to well-established habit (formed in the past), or we respond intelligently, in the moment. We relinquish the power over our emotions at our peril. That is a privilege we should reserve only for ourselves. As soon as we give it away by blaming someone for how we feel, we are rendered impotent to change it. If we can't have a say in how we feel, why should anyone else?

Secondly, we need to dispense with any concern we may have for what others think of us. This may sound outrageous at first, but the reality is that you will never know *exactly* how someone else perceives you - thanks to their point of view and blind spots - and even if you did, you have very limited influence over it. So best to stick to what you can control, and that is: what you think of yourself.

Thirdly, we need to maintain inner vigilance, noticing how to get in the gap between the trigger and the reaction, and call on our innate intelligence to give us real choice.

This approach is all about using ourselves as the frame of reference for decision-making, not something or someone else.

What does it look and feel like in practice?

Scenario 1

You are in your office when the door suddenly opens and your finance director - the one I mentioned earlier - breezes in and starts talking. You immediately feel a surge of indignation and anger well up in you. It starts from your stomach and quickly gets into your head - your blood pressure is rising fast. It's been a bad day so far and his interruption is the last straw.

That feeling is your reminder that you are being railroaded down the track of two choices: suppress and suffer or express and explode. The first will ensure a predictable outcome: no change. The second will make you feel better - short term - the fallout will be unpredictable.

But now you know there is a third way. You determine to respond, not react. You gather yourself and remember that you are in complete control of your response. You allow him to finish. You then pause for longer than usual. The silence is palpable. You explain that you will explore the issue with him at 4pm. Then you ask him to always ensure that he knocks on the door before entering, if it is closed. He looks a little sheepish, apologises and leaves, closing the door after him.

What you do not do is: externalise the emotions, explain yourself; refer to the past; criticise him or his behaviour; say anything that isn't respectful or polite. Consequently, you can rest easy knowing that whatever his reaction/response is, it is neither your fault, nor your responsibility.

You know from his reaction that he is likely to change his behaviour from now on. The feelings subside - you have acted on them, but on your terms. Note also that this response applies regardless of seniority.

Scenario 2

In today's executive board meeting, the sales director is up to his usual tricks. He's just closed a large sale and he's cockier than ever in his attempts to dominate the conversation.

Familiar feelings of frustration and irritation threaten to overwhelm you until you remember the real choice you have.

You call his name loudly. He stops and looks at you while you again let the silence do its work. You tell him that you have noted on several occasions this morning that he has interrupted his colleagues, talking over them and preventing them from having the space to express themselves. You ask that he desist from now on so others can add the value that he does in these meetings. Eye contact and more silence...

No personal criticism or hostility, just a simple request. No reference to the past and his long track record of obnoxious behaviour. And no betrayal of your visceral, internal reaction. You also turn your intervention into an opportunity to praise him, sincerely.

The result of the intervention - paradoxically - doesn't matter. What matters is that the truth is told in the moment.

Scenario 3

Your people director informs you that she can no longer work with her operations colleague, who apparently told the marketing director that the entire HR department was a waste of space and couldn't do its job. She is adamant that this is the last straw and that one of them has to go.

Hopefully you can see a pattern emerging that will enable you to pre-empt the right response to the conflict between your ops and people directors. The principles are very simple:

- Acknowledge how you feel to yourself

- Remember that any urge to react intemperately is just a learnt, negative habit from the past and has no place in an intelligent response.

- Judge the behaviour, not the person.

- State what is needed, clearly, positively and briefly, without emotion.

- Use silence and eye contact judiciously.

This sequence requires you to put out of your mind the outcome of the intervention. It's all about the moment, the now. You're being true to yourself and the situation, not directed by a flurry of emotion and fantasy over what might happen and what others think. Whatever the outcome, an intelligent intervention allows you to build on it until the result you want is achieved; reactions don't.

Now this scenario is different from the others, because the issue lies between people other than you. You are not directly involved. Their relationship is exactly that: their relationship, not yours. This is a crucial distinction, which we'll be examining later on in the book - one that the most senior and experienced leaders can get wrong.

Why are you not responsible for their relationship - even at work, as their line manager?

Because:

***They* are responsible for their relationship - no one else.**

Based on this principle, and those above, you explain to the people director that part of her job requirement is the ability to get on with all her colleagues. If she can't fulfil that need, she can't do her job. You say that you'll be telling the ops director exactly the same and that thereafter, you will hold them both responsible for their relationship. Any failure to maintain a mutually respectful, working relationship will mean you have to take action other than mediation.

Surprisingly, mediating between adults can often aggravate the relationship as either or both can use the mediator as protection for their positions and behaviour.

Governing one's behaviour in this way increases the options you have for constructive and creative interventions. Taking back control from visceral urges to correct others' behaviour, and using it to intelligently moderate your own, has powerful paybacks for leadership.

It also demonstrates behaviour that others will want to emulate - and in doing so will propagate it through the organisation creating a culture of good behaviour.

As Edmund in King Lear suggests in the opening quote, it's all too tempting to blame the stars - and others - when, in reality, the power for change lies with you.

•

Roundup

- Your behaviour is the result of the way in which you discipline and manage your conduct… or not

- Our frame of reference for the way we behave needs to be ours, not others' behaviour

- Acknowledging and feeling your emotions does not mean externalising them

- You are not responsible for anyone else's behaviour. Why? Because they are.

- The other person is not their behaviour. Judge behaviour, not the person.

INFLUENCE

I'll teach you how to flow

In 1936, Dale Carnegie wrote *How to Win Friends and Influence People*. It sold 15 million copies and in 2011, was number 19 on Time Magazine's list of the 100 most influential books.

The prospect of being able to influence others is magnetically attractive. Influence is power: just imagine being able to steer the direction in which others think and behave; the implications for your leadership, and the success of the organisation you lead, are immense.

Reading a book today on the same subject, you might expect to learn about a whole toolbox full of techniques for bending the way people think to your advantage: hypnosis, NLP (neuro-linguistic programming) and modelling, to name three. The boundary between influence and persuasion - or even manipulation - can be a fine one.

Yet, returning to Dale Carnegie's book, the emphasis is overwhelmingly not on changing the other person's behaviour, but on taking control of your own. The first two of his three principles for dealing with people are:

1. Do not criticise, condemn or complain.

2. Give honest and sincere appreciation.

Both of these require many of us to discipline our lower habits of mind and behaviour.

There is a totally counter-intuitive reality at the heart of true influence, and that is:

The best way to influence another person is not to try.

So if you want to exert some kind of influence over someone, how on earth do you do it?

The common understanding of having influence is all about getting people to listen to you. And yet the way you get people to listen to you, is by listening to them. Listening to others makes them feel valued by you, and strengthens the relationship between you. We all want to feel valued. We value people who value us. So, just as I suggest we change the things we *can* control, not those we can't, the best strategy for influencing others is through allowing them to influence you. That happens naturally by listening to them and valuing whatever they have to say.

Crucially, this is not about generating impressions, this is about taking a genuine, authentic and sincere interest in what other people want to say. And to do that you have to relinquish any idea of what you want in return. There is never space for both.

The very best listeners employ *non-judgemental curiosity* - a search for truth that excludes nothing and includes all.

Much has been written about the art of Active Listening, through which the listener - moving away from passivity - actively displays and confirms interest, engagement, empathy in, and understanding of whatever the speaker is imparting. As with all techniques though, the process can negate its benefit. Employing the tools of active listening - such as observing body language, reflecting, summarising etc. - can easily pull your attention away from its prime focus: listening.

Following your natural curiosity to understand what your colleagues think and feel - and withholding any urge to judge - is all the guidance you need, not only to understand, but to be *seen* to understand. Remaining still and present, clues and cues on how to interact as a listener will emerge quite naturally.

Any leader that does not genuinely feel curious towards the way their people think and feel, needs to question their position.

•

The word *influence* denotes a sense of flowing in from some external source - an influx. In a leadership context, that source is whoever you are communicating with. For them, the source is you. There is a mutual exchange or flow.

But what exactly is it that is flowing? At the physical level it is sound. Intellectually, it's an idea. Emotionally, a feeling. Is that it?

Let's look at the origin of the word *influence* in more detail:

According to etymological sources, the word originally referred to the flow of inspiration, authority or power from the stars. A flow of astral energy, if you like.

Now I am not, for a moment, suggesting that we ascribe any significance whatsoever to astrology - but perhaps this more expansive definition points to the impact of influence going beyond just the words we articulate.

One aspect of influence, which some people are able to transmit just by walking into a room, is that of *charisma*. Their very presence makes us feel different. Feeling different, we think and act differently. That is a result of influence, and yet no words have to be spoken. Sometimes the silence conveys more than words ever could.

Charismatic people are influential, though the reverse is not always the case.

Notwithstanding his politics or his fall from grace, ex-US president, Bill Clinton, has always been admired for his charisma. When asked, people who have met him talk of how he listens to them:

"…like you are the most important person he's talked to that day. Even though you know you're not, you still feel like you are."

And:

"He made me feel as if I was the only person in the room."

Videos of him talking to members of the public bear this out. He is able to channel his attention totally on the other person. They feel listened to; they feel valued.

Charisma though, whatever it is, is a tool that has no intrinsic morality. As the Indian mystic, Sadhguru, points out:

"People who lead with charisma can lead people to disasters. We want people who lead with good sense. You will see the greatest things in the world are being done – truly things of absolute human importance are being done – not necessarily by charismatic people. They are being done by sensible people who know what to do and what not to do."

So, in influence and charisma we have qualities, which can change the way people feel. If decision-making is based on how we feel (as we saw in chapter 2.1) then these qualities can change the way we act and behave.

And if charisma is a quality, which can be felt beyond the influence of words - perhaps by presence alone - then as leaders, we need to be tuned in to what we transmit.

The idea of influence at a distance is not far removed from Einstein's description of Quantum Entanglement as "spooky action at a distance". He was referring to a property of decaying atoms in which the *spin* of a particle is 'known' by its counterpart both instantaneously and at a distance. The inference is that information is transferred between them in no time at all, in total defiance of Einstein's theory of special relativity, which states that nothing travels faster than the speed of light.

Quantum Entanglement has since been verified as a genuine phenomenon and is currently a focus of research into Quantum Computing.

Is it possible that the ability to shape people's feelings, and therefore their actions, can take place beyond our everyday understanding of influence?

Could the way we think and feel *internally* impact others, without any overt, external expression?

Yogic science takes this as a given. It holds *sangha* - company - as a key influence in one's life. Regardless of your behaviour, the behaviour of those around has an impact upon you. Yogic philosophy is clear that most human beings are – knowingly or unknowingly – shaped by the company that they keep.

Jim Rohn - the American entrepreneur - expressed this rather more bluntly (and possibly less accurately) in this soundbite: "You are the average of the five people you spend the most time with."

Notice again how - in the search for clarity on this subject of influence - the emphasis has shifted from others, to yourself: the influences we embrace shape the influence we have on those we lead. Or as John Donne, the Elizabethan poet, put it:

"No man is an island entire of itself; every man is a piece of the continent, a part of the main;"

John Maxwell, the author and speaker on leadership, is unequivocal: "Leadership *is* influence" - and although undeniable, within this statement lies a trap.

If, as good leaders, we try to influence - we make influence the focus of our leadership - we immediately fall flat on our faces. The same, or even worse, goes for charisma - as soon as you try to be charismatic, you immediately become the opposite. And if you don't believe me, please go ahead and try.

The reason that trying to be influential or charismatic always fails is because of the shift you make in your frame of reference. It shifts from self-reference, to some abstract notion of what someone else may need to be influenced by you, or to perceive you as charismatic. Frequently it shifts you towards copying other peoples' behaviours. This shift takes you away from what you are, to what you are not. It is inauthentic and lacks integrity, wholeness.

Influence comes through maintaining your inner frame of reference whilst opening yourself up to the influence of others and responding accordingly. You may or may not be considered charismatic as a result. Neither is your concern.

•

Roundup

- Influence is about a flow of energy

- The best way to influence someone is to open yourself to influence

- Charisma is dangerous without good sense

- Prioritise good influences for yourself over trying to influence others

- What others think of you is not your concern

Give Up and Let Go

When vice makes mercy, mercy's so extended, That for the fault's love is the offender friended.

In The Lion King there is a scene in which Rafiki the monkey hits Simba the lion over the head with his stick. "OW! Geez, what was that for?!" says Simba. Rafiki replies: "It doesn't matter! It's in the past!"

Rafiki (Swahili for friend) is demanding that Simba immediately let go of any bad feeling associated with the action. Not in due course - right now.

Rafiki swings his stick again. This time Simba ducks and the stick misses.

In our everyday, reactive mode of thinking, we might well encourage Simba to blame Rafiki for his sore head. Some might even suggest that Simba wreak revenge or retribution: an eye for an eye, a tooth for a tooth. Getting justice is the first port of call for many who have been wronged.

Yet, notwithstanding his headache, Simba has learnt something: stay alert and get out of the way if you see a stick coming at you. Perhaps he also learns that *real* friends aren't there to always make you feel good. He may also have seen, whatever the event, how you react is your responsibility, no one else's. That's a lot of learning from a real friend!

Find some quiet time to do the following exercise: Cast your mind back to an event in which you were apparently disadvantaged by someone else's action. Maybe you lost out on a promotion due to a colleague's intervention. Perhaps one of your team messed up and you had to take the heat. Maybe someone deliberately undermined you, at work or in your personal life. Or a boss continually encouraged you with prospects of great opportunities that never materialised. Or what about the accident that changed the course of your life?

Does it still rankle? If not, find something that does - something you still carry around with you as unfinished business. Don't delude yourself that there is nothing.

When you've identified something, immerse yourself in it, re-live it and feel the emotions associated with it. Painful? Good.

Blame should hurt. Whether or not it hurts anyone else, who knows. But it will hurt the blamer. The reason it hurts is because:

Blame is a denial of power - your power.

The word blame has the same roots as the word *blaspheme* which is the denial of divine power. Blame renders you impotent and that's always going to hurt.

What's the antidote to blame? Firstly, think of blame, metaphorically, as a burden or load that you're carrying around with you. Feel the emotional weight of it. It's not a part of you, it's something that you have decided to carry with you. Just as you have decided to carry it, you can decide to put it down. Try it: in your imagination, put the burden of blame down on the ground and walk away from it.

Now, being totally honest with yourself, determine whether or not you *really* want to offload and abandon the blame. If you do, you're well on the way. If you don't, read on.

One of the biggest obstacles to shedding the judgement of blame towards others is the notion of *forgiveness*.

The common perception of forgiveness is as an act of mercy towards another. You forgive them some misdemeanour, some error of judgement. You let them off the hook or even let them get away with whatever they did. You absolve them of sin. You are *giving* something to them, which they may not deserve.

This understanding is not only mistaken but utterly degenerate. It also stands in the way of our wellbeing.

True forgiveness has nothing to do with anyone but you. To forgive means *to give up*. It refers to the giving up of blame. By forgiving, you're not doing anyone else any favours. You're not cleansing them of sin - that's their job, not yours.

Your job is to take responsibility for how you respond to any situation and not pass it off onto another. If, instead, you choose to blame someone else, you'll have to carry that blame around with you wherever you go, even when you're not thinking about it. What they do with the blame is down to them.

Some of us turn others' blame into our guilt. Guilt, or self-blame - is a form of self-harm and just another load for us to carry around and weigh us down. You can deal with it in the same way as blame. Forgive it - put it down and abandon it. It serves no useful purpose - quite the opposite, it's corrosive and toxic. Blame requires you to harbour anger, resentment and bitterness. These are the arsenic, strychnine and cyanide of the mind.

Make no mistake: true forgiveness is something we do for ourselves. How others deal with any blame or judgement we put on them is down to them. But clearly all our relationships can only improve if we determine to give up and let go of blame, guilt and all the other judgements that impact negatively on us. The clue is always in our feelings.

Forgiving does not mean forgetting. To forget is to lose the power of recalling to mind. Another loss of power. So, by all means forgive, but never forget. Remember what happened and refrain from blaming.

A strategy, which can be very tempting to employ, is that of trying to forget without forgiving. In essence, this is emotional suppression, which only comes back to bite us at some future point in time. Many behavioural disorders and addictions are fuelled by unresolved, suppressed emotion. Furthermore, there is evidence to suggest that suppression is not only ineffective, but counter-productive.

A study in 1987 on this topic involved one group of people who were told not to think about a white bear. Another group was allowed to think about anything, including a white bear. The group that suppressed thoughts of a white bear ended up having more white bear thoughts than the group that had been allowed to think freely.

This is called the rebound effect of thought suppression. When you suppress thoughts on a topic, you end up having more thoughts on that same topic. The same is true for suppression of emotions.

A powerful precept is to both forgive and remember everything that happens to us in our lives - the quicker we forgive, the better we get at it and the happier we stay.

Great leadership demands the ability to forgive quickly and completely - never to forget.

•

Roundup

- Blame is a load that *you* carry - not the person you're blaming

- You have no right to absolve anyone else of their sins - only they can do that

- Forgive wholeheartedly, but never forget

- Forgetting without forgiving is merely suppression

- To blame is to surrender your power to change

Say No... Often

No

The concept of No is intrinsic to the world we live in, as is its opposite, Yes.

Is this a table? No, it's a book.

Yes and No define boundaries. Physically, we know things through their boundaries - their edges. The walls of our office determine whether or not we are at work - or they used to. Our skin defines where our bodies start and end. The Earth's horizon controls night and day as the Sun rises and sets.

Remove all boundaries and we are left with a homogenous soup, lacking definition and difference - a chaotic, entropic mess.

As leaders, Yes and No create the edges and boundaries in our organisations and lives, which bring order and system.

Yes and No are just two sides of the same coin. They form a mutually exclusive dichotomy, which cannot co-exist. Logically, they are equal and opposite. But emotionally they are not -

No has an image problem.

Say No... Often

Nice people say Yes - selfish people say No. Positive people like to say Yes and apologise for occasionally having to say No. Perhaps the Positive Thinking movement is responsible. Or maybe the 1980s car part supplier's slogan: "The answer's Yes. Now what's the question?"

Annie is the Marketing Director of an online travel company employing several thousand staff, internationally. She is very talented, highly creative and the way she leads her division is the envy of her fellow directors. She is a high-achiever in every respect.

Everybody likes Annie - she is bright, positive, friendly, helpful and always has time for you. Even though she has a lot on her plate, nothing is too much trouble.

As a child, Annie quickly got used to taking responsibility when her single mother developed a life-changing illness. She remembers the gratitude her mum and sisters would show for the way she would take the initiative to make sure everything was taken care of. Her teachers, aware of the situation, would praise her sense of duty. The appreciation from others gave her a powerful buzz of satisfaction.

At work, she was the go-to person for anyone with a problem. She epitomised the saying "If you want something done, ask a busy person.". Whether it was a technical, commercial or a people problem - even a personal one, Annie would help.

Every request was accepted with a smile and a Yes. Often, Annie would pre-empt the request and intervene without being asked - always helpful, forever selfless.

Meanwhile, those that showed less appreciation took second place - her family in particular. The relationship with her husband deteriorated and her adolescent children started to play up at school. The more criticism she felt at home, the more she gravitated to the one place that made her feel good: work.

To any opportunity that promised a hit of recognition and thanks, she would say: Yes. Her family, in contrast to her work, withdrew their appreciation as she withdrew her attention.

Last year, Annie took six months stress-related leave after having been found walking down the local high street in her dressing gown and slippers, in a distressed state. It was a wake-up call for her, her family and her employer.

During the period of recovery Annie learnt a lot about herself. She realised that she had developed a dependency on others' appreciation. This had started in childhood and she had not grown out of it. The need for people's esteem had become addictive and she subconsciously shunned any environment that didn't give her that fulfilment.

Friends and colleagues urged her to focus on her work-life balance and her time management. But she knew the resolution went much deeper than just re-organising her outer world.

Annie's real breakthrough was realising that she couldn't depend on *any* external source of gratification - it had to come from within. So just trying to squeeze more appreciation out of her family and less out of work, wouldn't address the root cause, only the symptoms. She had to become emotionally independent.

Her time away from work allowed Annie to deepen her self-awareness and to sensitise herself to her inner dynamics - how her thinking and feeling worlds, her learnt behaviours, habits, beliefs and identity, play together to create her experience. She saw how her feelings were not, in reality, a result of the people around her, but a direct consequence of how she used her mind.

Returning to work, she was able to start making decisions based on what was best for the business and her colleagues, not on any need for appreciation. The change was astounding. Colleagues soon discovered that the old Annie who would take on anything they asked of her, would now say No unless the case for her input was cast-iron. She also became adept at delegation.

Today, Annie works 9-5, very rarely at the weekends. She spends much more time with her family, which she enjoys and they appreciate. Her relationship with her children and husband is better than she could ever have imagined. She knows that this is all down to her simple decision never to rely on anyone else to feel good - which means that she can't blame anyone for making her feel bad either. Because she tries to take responsibility for how she feels, she feels great most of the time.

Far from becoming emotionally isolated from her loved ones, this new approach has brought them all closer together.

Annie also realises that taking on someone else's responsibility - even if it seems helpful - is the worst thing you can do for them. It denies them their *ability to respond,* and displaces your own responsibility. She sees very clearly how her need to be liked drove her to interfere with other people's development and to neglect her own.

People still like Annie, but they have a respect for her now that was lacking before. They think twice about disturbing her. For her part, Annie no longer cares what other people think about her. She is always friendly and polite but she knows that whatever others may think, it's not really her concern. She's no longer a girl who can't say No.

Another profound shift that Annie made during her recovery was the realisation that she is not responsible for her people. She enjoys telling others this stark fact and waiting for the inevitable question: "How come? You're the boss - if you aren't responsible for them, who is?" To which she answers: "T*hey* are responsible for themselves, just like every adult on the planet." She goes on to explain that her role is to create an environment in which all her people can take as much responsibility as they choose.

This particular shift required her to re-jig her senior team, some of whom had become used to Annie spoon-feeding them. Two of them found difficulty in stepping up to her new modus operandi and left within a few months. Annie realised how her former behaviour was responsible and she was so grateful that the rest of the team adapted quickly.

Annie has stopped:

> Defaulting to Yes
>
> Offering an opinion without being asked
>
> Saying what people *should* do
>
> Giving unsolicited advice
>
> Taking challenges away from people

Annie will still intervene when the situation demands, but it's because she finds herself tuned into her colleagues and able to see their real needs much more clearly, unmuddied by her own subconscious urges.

At home, she has adopted exactly the same approach. Because she no longer expects her husband to take responsibility for her domestic happiness, her equanimity has improved their relationship beyond recognition. Now she no longer depends on his behaviour to feel happy, they both feel freer to behave naturally and spontaneously - making them both happier and lighter in the process. They work as a team and their children's problems are rapidly abating.

The paradox that: making yourself less dependent on others, brings them closer to you, does not escape her - but it does mean that she is very selective with whom she opens up to. Not everybody gets it. She is also very aware of how the same principles operate equally at home and at work. There is no difference - both are just different aspects of the same life.

When Annie is not sure of what to do, she'll wait to see how her inner guidance systems behave before committing to action. Sometimes she'll take a decision without being quite certain if it's the right one, but not before giving it space and time in her mind.

The intention behind her actions has undergone a seismic shift. She is still highly valued at work, but no longer as a *White Knight* riding in to save everyone from their problems.

Not all of us have trouble saying No - some of us prefer it to Yes. The point is that the best answer to any request lies within us, in that space between the thinking and the feeling, which the request generates. The less calm, clear and quiet we are, the more likely our frame of reference will be mood, habit, or belief - all of which are fickle products of the past. That's not to say the past has no relevance, simply that its dominance will leave us at the mercy of what has been, not what is.

•

Roundup

Say No... Often

- No is the opposite of Yes - it is not intrinsically negative

- Yes and No used in balance create boundaries, vital in life, relationships and organisations

- When boundaries are not well-defined and respected, unwanted behaviours can creep in and take root

- Seemingly positive behaviour can mask pathological thinking

- A calm, clear mind always promotes the right response

Speaking and Listening

Give every man thy ear but few thy voice. Take each man's censure but reserve thy judgment.

Speaking and listening are acts of communication that form the foundation of our relationships. We speak to transmit ideas; we listen to receive them, and be moved by the feelings they evoke. This form of communication uses sound as the medium, and is subject to several translations: an idea is articulated into a language - the words are transformed into physical vibrations through speech - the speech is heard and retranslated back into words, and once more into ideas. We can summarise this as:

$$\text{Meaning} \rightarrow \text{Sound} \rightarrow \text{Meaning}$$

The process is phenomenally complex and sophisticated - and that's just the physics. Every link in the chain has to work. A foreign language, roadworks, a thick accent, a bad telephone line can all easily prevent understanding. By design, enough redundancy is built into the process to ensure that genuine *mis*understanding is far less common than *lack* of understanding.

The intellectual gymnastics that ensue are even more extraordinary. Electrical signals from the inner ear become words in mind, the words become thoughts, concepts, propositions, opinions, all of which are then assessed for meaning, intention and inference.

All manner of obstacles, which line up to derail the meaning, are generally navigated with ease, including: idiom, culture, metaphor and context.

When an artificial intelligence engine translates the expression "Out of sight, out of mind" as: "The invisible lunatic", or "The spirit was willing, but the flesh was weak" as: "The vodka was good but the steak was lousy", our amusement is fuelled by the knowledge of just how intricate, refined and highly developed the process of communication is.

Happily, we can leave most of the processing to our sensory and cognitive faculties which evolved during childhood, and hopefully continue to do so.

Once the meaning is captured, we can then let our power of discrimination and judgement loose on the message. This can happen just as automatically and predictably as everything that preceded it. Our identity, memory and intellect are only too willing to dissect the meaning, compare it to our standards, and defend our position by agreeing with it, or dismissing it.

This is where the process of communication can most easily breakdown. Rather than allowing the time and space for real understanding to emerge, we can so easily intervene to prevent the insight that is available.

When we listen to someone, the message is just one small component of the whole picture.

In contrast with the physical aspect of listening, in this realm, misunderstanding is more common than a lack of understanding.

All of this begs the question: How do we connect with the deepest possible understanding? How do we transform the data into information, knowledge, even wisdom?

The answer is very simple but not always so easy to practise:

Conscious listening creates understanding

What this means is that the listening itself does everything you need in order to understand. You have to do nothing but listen. No thinking, processing, evaluating, judging, taking notes, comparing, liking or waiting to reply - just listening.

To listen, we temporarily suspend the workings of our judgement machine, and open ourselves to connect with the fullest possible meaning from whatever is being expressed. At this point we can also embrace not just the sound of communication but also the visual cues including expression, posture, movements, eye contact - not in order to interpret, which is an intellectual function, but to understand.

Paying attention in this way does not seem to come naturally to many of us. We are so practised at encouraging our intellects to intervene, that the noise drowns out the innate intelligence of listening. But when we do just listen, the effect transforms not just our experience of understanding, but also the speakers experience of being listened to - of being valued through listening.

Relearning this skill is really a matter of unlearning a whole load of superfluous activity. It's about doing less, not more. Here are some pointers:

- Use the sound of the speaker's voice as your focus.

- When you notice a distraction - the urge to reply, a criticism, another sound - just return to the focal point.

- Let the speaker finish before responding.

- Leave a silence before speaking.

- Reflect back and summarise before you move on to your point - or ask for clarification.

This process is not dissimilar to that of meditation. We're not asking our mind to stop working, we're just not allowing it to intervene on its terms.

All this can take place very naturally with the usual little signs of appreciation - a nod, a 'yes', a smile. Take care with reflecting back - summarising what you've heard needs to avoid sounding like a therapist! Practise and get better.

Actively disciplining and prioritising your listening in this way will make speaking more concise and effective.

Emma has two managers who are not getting on with each other. There is clear antipathy between them that is not getting any better. Emma invites them both to a meeting. She asks Rob to describe exactly what is going on in his opinion, whilst Ava listens and remains silent. Emma listens too but also asks questions to clarify and reflect back. The meeting ends without any input from Ava. The next day the tables are turned. This time Ava speaks, Rob listens and Emma once again listens, clarifies and reflects. Rob is silent for the whole meeting.

The following day, Emma convenes a final meeting in which she asks Ava and Rob to just listen to her. She explains that now that both of them have spoken, and been listened to, she expects them to find a way forward in their relationship. She tells them that she will not intervene in their relationship again, but should it remain an issue, it could impact on their continued employment.

The relationship immediately improved. Rob and Ava never became best buddies, but they found a way of cooperating. The fact of being held responsible for their relationship certainly helped, but in Emma's words: "This was the first time each of them had actually heard what the other thought and felt, clearly and calmly. Being heard was more important than being right. The fact neither was able to react in the moment allowed the feelings to subside overnight and not interfere in the listening."

Listening is not a passive activity - ever. It is the act of giving your attention to the other person as fully as possible. Your attention or awareness is, in reality, all you can give to anyone at any time. If you have any doubt as to the veracity of that fact, try thinking, listening, speaking or doing anything without attention.

Speaking and Listening

The original meaning of the word communication, was to *make common*. Clearly, listening is only part of the equation, even if we are urged to listen more than we speak.

Superficially, speaking is a more sophisticated activity than listening. We have to marshal all our thoughts, articulate them and lay ourselves open to misinterpretation, disagreement, conflict - even indifference. We need to be clear on what we are trying to communicate, how we do it and why. No such problem with listening. Often, the underlying mix of emotion, desire and motivation behind the message may be far more complex than the words themselves.

The common metaphor for speaking to someone is that of injecting ideas into their head. Unfortunately, nothing could be further from the truth. Understanding is always a function of the culture, experience, intellect, learning and emotions, which both of you bring to the conversation - never just what you mean.

We've all experienced how it feels to be second-guessing our listener by using guarded language, euphemisms, metaphors and figures of speech that leave them, and you, not quite sure of just how the message landed.

The simplest and most effective way to bypass all the factors that can derail understanding, and to connect with your innate intelligence is through listening. Listening both when the other is speaking, and when you are speaking.

Listening to the sound of your own voice - in the same way as you listen to other voices, outlined above, is a very powerful way of speaking. Oddly, perhaps, you can do this without interference to your flow of words. Often, the flow improves as a result.

I recommend that you try it, practise it and perfect it. Use the sounds that you make whilst you are speaking as the focal point of your attention. You will still be able to maintain eye contact, and notice the other person's behaviour, but your attention will be on your voice.

•

Roundup

- Conscious listening creates understanding

- Focus on the sound of the voice - yours and theirs

- Being heard is often more important to us than being right

- Use silence as well as sound when speaking

- Use eye contact consciously

PART 4
THE COMPLETE LEADER

Exploring the personal and relationship aspects of leadership naturally leads us to examine the practical business of leading others as a complete, rather than a broken leader.

In Charles Dickens' *A Christmas Carol* we witness the transformation of a "squeezing, wrenching, grasping, scraping, clutching, covetous, old sinner" into "as good a friend, as good a master, and as good a man, as the good old city knew". Admittedly, the change was facilitated supernaturally, but it was the insights into his own self, which transformed Scrooge - not any external agent.

In our non-fictional world, personal, relationship and leadership transformation is likely to be incremental rather than drastic - though each insight is often sudden and radical in its feeling and impact.

The transformation into a complete leader is therefore an evolution - an unfolding - of what is already there. But to make way for what can be, we have to discard much of what is - rather like the butterfly shedding its chrysalis. Herein lies another paradox - or at least a challenge to the received wisdom - that leadership is so often about doing less rather than more.

It's also about finding the optimal point of balance between extremes. The physicist, Ernest Rutherford, led his team to no fewer than eight Nobel prizes under the directive: "See what's inside the atom." Defined as a *medium-level abstraction* (MLA) this kind of statement finds the sweet spot between overly nebulous edicts such as "Don't be evil" and highly specific instruction which, by attempting to minimise risk, also strangles creative collaboration, serendipity and synchronicity.

The beauty and bane of leadership is that, in its truest form, and whatever the context - global corporation or domestic duty - its finest expression is found in the moment, free of beliefs, mindsets and opinions. Simply an inner feeling, informed by reason, illuminating the next step.

In the 80s, James Carse described finite games in which the player has to move from one game to another as soon as it is complete. The objective is to win. There is a winner and a loser and the game is played within boundaries and rules. Examples include sport, political elections and war.

In an infinite game, everything is very different. Players come and go, rules change and there is no endpoint - the objective is to keep playing. Life is an infinite game. As leaders we can play either a finite or an infinite game. In *The Infinite Game*, Simon Sinek writes about how the majority of businesses play a finite game and suffer the consequences: "The minute you have senior executives obsessing about the short game, the game is lost."

Purpose defines the game you're playing. If your purpose is to outperform the competition, you're playing a finite game. If your purpose is to increase shareholder ROI, you're playing a finite game. If it's to double market capitalisation through acquisition, you're playing a finite game.

So how do you play the infinite game as a leader? You play to stay in the game so that you can continue to deliver your value to the world.

That is the only true purpose a leader can have.

DELEGATING TRUST

Love all, trust a few, Do wrong to none

When former four-star general, Colin Powell, was asked: How would you define the key characteristics of leadership? He answered without thought or hesitation with one word: Trust.

Trust is fundamental to any transaction or exchange of value. Any lack of trust in your relationship with another will either distort the transaction or block it completely. Trust in the brand is an overarching priority for today's marketers and influencers.

A prime function of leadership is facilitating transactions with others and between others. I'm not just talking about the exchange of goods for services or products, I'm referring to every conversation, decision, intention, delegation, vision and process. Business is a wholly transactional activity.

We don't need definitions here - we are all intimately connected with trust at a visceral level. We feel it, and we feel the lack of it. Trust helps us feel secure, but the inconvenient paradox is that we have to make ourselves vulnerable to experience it. That vulnerability feels like the antithesis of the security, which trust is meant to deliver.

Vulnerability, which facilitates the flow of trust, is critical to not just healthy leadership, but also to scalable growth of the organisation.

The most common impediment to trust, which I witness in organisations, is *fake* trust masquerading as the real thing. It manifests through:

Delegating activity without responsibility

This type of leadership covers a wide spectrum of behaviours, from intrusive micromanagement at one end, to setting people up to fail at the other.

The mechanics of it are very simple and particularly frequent amongst owner-managers and entrepreneurs.

Hans runs a gaming tech company, which he founded six years ago. Hans is gifted, to put it mildly. He has a double first in Maths from Oxford, speaks five languages fluently and had made his first million by the time he was 24 years old. He could have been a virtuoso violinist if he'd wanted.

His company then employed 180 people and at 35 he could live on his yacht and sail the world for the rest of his life if he chose. But Hans was not happy. The company, in his view, was underperforming and so were his people. His senior team were showing increasing signs of disengagement and, at times, incompetence.

When I asked him who he would re-employ if his whole team resigned on a Friday and asked for their jobs back on the Monday, he said no one. He would have no compunction firing them all, but he could not find replacements.

His people were very well-paid, incentivised and resourced, yet they didn't seem to take the initiative when needed and they certainly didn't take responsibility. The company strategy was crystal clear - he delegated every action behind the strategic objectives to each of his directors. They knew exactly what to do, but the execution was not even mediocre, it was downright deficient.

When I spoke to his marketing director, Sam, I got a very different picture: Hans is a control freak. Hans has a finger in every pie. He involves himself in every decision and every action - he breathes down the necks of everyone in the business. No one can do or say anything without Hans knowing and intervening.

Sam and his colleagues have told Hans about their grievance in no uncertain terms. The non-execs have told Hans. His best friend has told him. But Hans always come back with the same riposte: "Show me I can trust you and I will."

Hans has created a Catch-22 bind for himself and the entire company. He is waiting for trustworthy behaviour from people he doesn't trust. He fails completely to understand that the trust comes from him, not from them. He needs certainty and sees vulnerability as a weakness.

Pointing to the delegation of tasks as proof of his willing to show partial trust, he misses the point that you either trust someone, or you don't - it's a binary condition.

His intellectual capability makes the situation worse. He behaves as he does, because he can - the company is making plenty of money and it's all down to him. He shows no sign of wanting to change.

Two years later, little has changed. The headcount is slightly down, as are profits, but the business is still financially sound. The senior team looks very different now. Those directors, including Sam, who found the most difficulty in working for Hans, have left. Others have got used to his management style and accept it. The same is largely true for the remainder of the workforce.

Hans himself has aged visibly, the long-term stress of doing so much and being personally responsible has taken its toll. But Hans is on a mission, and he never gives up. He's not going to change for anyone or anything...

In summary: Hans delegates activity, but not the responsibility that goes with it. He retains that for himself - after all, it's his business. It's too risky to let people off the leash - no one has proved themselves capable of taking on that responsibility - he cannot jeopardise the success of the company just to indulge in some pink and fluffy thinking around trust. Trust has to be earned.

Hans' thinking creates an organisation that is wholly dependent on him and his capacity to work. It grows to a certain size and flatlines there because it is inherently not scalable. This kind of organisation attracts people who need to be told what to do at every turn, and it repels self-starters, innovators and high-achievers. It also subjects Hans himself to very high levels of stress, which are not sustainable.

The alternative to how Hans runs his company is to extend trust to everyone you employ, as a matter of course. You do so by delegating both the activity *and the responsibility*, which goes with it. To separate the two and to retain responsibility is a fear-based act, which demeans both parties, creating stress, frustration and anxiety in its wake. Perversely, in trying to avoid the stress of uncertainty by eschewing vulnerability, far more stress is created as a result.

Once again we see how our inner belief-system creates the world we experience and how intervention only at the causal level is effective.

The example also demonstrates how using financials as the sole indicator of success can exacerbate a fundamentally unhealthy situation and sustain dysfunctional leadership.

Leaders who delegate activity *and* responsibility are making themselves vulnerable to others. To delegate is to literally *untie* someone or set them free. Only then can that person deliver to the peak of their potential - anything else and they are destined to underperform.

In this way, trust sets people free in a way that nothing else can - and just as Colin Powell intimated:

Trust is the first act of leadership

Charlie, an owner-manager, took this fear of trust one stage further than most. He would, without being fully aware of what he was doing, set his directors up to fail so that he could be fully justified in constantly complaining about how untrustworthy they were.

He would allow his technical director to pursue courses of action that he knew would fail, and not intervene. He would wait for mistakes from other directors to have the maximum impact on the business before holding them to account. You can imagine that the people he retained were not always of the highest calibre, so it was a bit like shooting fish in a barrel.

It is difficult to imagine someone with a business at stake to behave in this way. Yet he got what he wanted out of it - he was always right. His experience confirmed his thinking that everyone around him was incompetent and that the trust he put in people was always abused. He was also desperately unhappy and stressed to the point of ill-health. Fortunately for all concerned, he sold the business and retired.

The complete leader creates an environment of trust and support in which the individual can develop their powers of responsibility and meet more and more of their potential.

•

Roundup

- Trust is the basis of leadership
- Without trust there is no collaboration

Delegating Trust

- Delegation means to unleash or unchain

- Trust is the ultimate enabler and motivator

- Delegating trust means delegating activity *and* responsibility

NOT TELLING BUT COACHING

We know what we are, but not what we may be.

Why would you tell someone you trust what to do? Surely, you can trust their judgement to know what to do? Or in the words of Steve Jobs, the late boss of Apple:

"It doesn't make sense to hire smart people and tell them what to do; we hire smart people so they can tell *us* what to do."

For smart, I also read *trusted*. Either way, why would you employ anyone who you have to tell what to do and how to do it? Of course we may well need to train them up but ultimately we need employees who are better than we are at what they do.

If there is any truth in this, it must follow that telling someone what to do demonstrates a lack of trust. And if trust really is the first act of leadership, then telling is not leading.

So what is the complete leader to do? Fortunately, the world of coaching gives us a few clues, should we need them.

Coaching is a Victorian metaphor, said to have been first coined in Oxford, referring to those tutors who "carried" their students through exams. Today, executive or leadership coaches purport not so much to carry their clients, but to get them to their destination faster. My own coaching practice offers *accelerated* evolution or development - another reference to movement.

The emphasis, in an executive coaching relationship, is very much on facilitating the client to find their own answers, insights and resolutions, rather than providing them, through telling.

Some years ago a study was made of toddlers comparing their differences in response to being given a teaspoon, as opposed to finding a teaspoon. The results showed that those who found teaspoons lying around would spend more time investigating them, or playing with them, than those who had been given the spoon.

Rather like the child who is more interested in the wrapping than the present inside, discovering something that is not being expressly provided seems to naturally generate more engagement.

I suggested in a previous chapter that the responsibility of leadership is to create an environment in which others can take on responsibility. Coaching facilitates this shift by asking questions of the client and getting them to find the answers, even leaving them unanswered in preference to telling. Quite apart from the fact that many of the questions, which a good leader and coach would ask, can *only* be answered by the client or employee, never another.

Let's take an example to shed some light on the matter:

Libby, your technical director, asks for your input on the question of whether or not to shutdown a research project, which she thinks cannot show any return on investment in the foreseeable future. Your first thought is to veto any idea of stopping it, in no uncertain terms - you see every sign that it will come good and pay a handsome dividend sooner rather than later. But as you've just finished this book, you think twice and enjoy a reflective silence instead.

"That's an interesting comment, Libby" you say, "what is leading you to that decision?" You decide to suspend all judgement and unleash your curiosity. You tease out of Libby all the data supporting her thesis, none of which are particularly persuasive.

"Are there any other factors at play here? What are the team dynamics like?" you ask. You just listen and sense she's a little more defensive on this subject. After some more gentle, but persistent questioning you discover that one of her team is proving to be less than responsive - borderline subversive, even.

"That sounds like quite a challenge, Libby - how are you dealing with it?" She says she doesn't know and gets visibly anxious talking about it. "Well, what are the actions you could take if you wanted - no holds barred - from summary dismissal to promotion?" You introduce absurdity, not to lighten the mood, but to show Libby that nothing will be excluded for now.

Not Telling But Coaching

"I think he needs talking to." she says. You ask if she's already had a word, to which she says "No, I don't think I'm the right person." You can see her point - Matt is nearing retirement and is considered an authority in his field. He can be truculent and recalcitrant. "Can you take him to one side, please?" She asks. You quietly relish the opportunity to say No, explaining that it's not your responsibility, it's hers.

You ask her how she might approach a chat with him, if she decided to. She hesitates and doesn't know where to start. You divert her attention to more mundane matters like: when might you do it and where?

After more than an hour of talking to Libby, she resolves, of her own volition, free of any compulsion, to have a conversation with Matt about his behaviour and the impact it's having on the team. At no point did you direct her other than to decline the invitation to talk to Matt yourself, enabling her to implement, and own, her suggestion. Through your skilful questioning, she's achieved sufficient clarity to go ahead.

She leaves your office visibly more positive and ready to face Matt, in spite of having no idea what the outcome will be.

The time you've invested will be well worth it, as you've opened the door for Libby to be more proactive in her leadership generally. You've also given her a live demonstration of coaching, which she can only benefit from and use with others.

Clearly this is not the last conversation of this nature that you have with Libby. Short term she starts to seek your input more frequently, even though all you do is ask questions and never seem to answer any! You notice that she is having more conversations, 1-on-1, with her team - she tells you that they are rather like the ones she has with you.

You notice that she displays more confidence in her leadership which even reflects in her posture.

Eventually you ask her how it went with Matt. "Oh, I just asked him how someone who was so highly esteemed in his field, and respected in the industry, could behave like a stroppy teenager at work. He went bright red and couldn't reply so I asked him how he would handle someone who was highly talented and valued, but sometimes difficult to get on with. He's been as good as gold since."

You then ask what moved her to have a conversation, which she was initially keen to avoid. She replies that it was the clarity of seeing her resistance as separate from herself. She had seen herself as non-confrontational and believed that to be a good part of who she was - her identity. Seeing how this behaviour was encouraging Matt's confrontational style, she realised she could still be her true self *and* adopt behaviour to suit the situation. She saw how retaining that belief about who she was made her part of the problem - as much a part as Matt!

Confrontation and non-confrontation are both perfectly suitable leadership styles to adopt in appropriate circumstances. However, they both make very bad identities as they then lock you into behavioural patterns, which you can't adapt to the situation because you *are* them. This is true for the vast majority of leadership styles.

What behaviours do you identify with, which limit your leadership potential?

Although using creative questions to facilitate people's development is a powerful leadership skill, we can't apply it to every circumstance that arises. Frequently, situations will need an immediate intervention - right now - without any time for the luxury of a more reflective approach. If the fire alarm goes off, a meeting to discuss it might be deemed not just inappropriate, but downright dangerous.

Rather like the response to a medical condition, such as chronic tonsillitis, might involve three different interventions:

Short Term:	Pain killers
Medium Term:	Antibiotics
Long Term:	Surgery

so can leadership interventions take largely three forms:

Short Term:	Techniques
Medium Term:	Strategies
Long Term:	Insights

In Libby's case, had the relationship between Matt and Libby broken down completely, you might well have chosen to apply a short term remedy - a pain killer - by speaking directly to Matt. You may also have told Matt and Libby to employ certain conflict management techniques and tactics to allow them to maintain enough civility to work together.

Alternatively, with the luxury of more time, you may have opted to put Matt on an anger management course in the hope that he would get to the root of his issues and deal with them. Another strategy would have been to employ a mediator to help both parties improve their relationship.

The approach you adopted obviated the need for techniques and strategies. You provided Libby with a catalyst for insight. As a direct result of your questioning, she began to see how her own internal dynamics, in the form of beliefs and mindsets, were limiting her behaviour to habitual reactions and blocking intelligent responses. She was able to see herself as part of the issue, not just Matt. She took responsibility and changed the situation.

Although techniques and strategies are sometimes necessary, they are never sufficient. Ultimately, only self-awareness will give us the insights needed for this kind of transformation.

•

Roundup

- Telling erodes trust - coaching promotes it

- Coaching engages intelligence - telling circumvents it

- Coaching focuses on facilitating insight but can also offer techniques and strategies when required

- Coaching is to telling as offering is to giving

- Coaching promotes conscious, personal choice over learnt, habitual reactions

CHAOS AND STASIS

And when I love thee not Chaos is come again.

If you've ever been surfing, you'll know the initial challenge is finding the right place to catch the wave. Even if you haven't, you'll know that too far out at sea, the waves are not doing that much - too far inshore, the waves have broken; it's too late.

The point at which the wave starts to break is the place to be. It's the edge of chaos - between the stasis of the open ocean and the entropy of the broken wave. The surfer seeks out this zone to ride the wave and have fun. This window of opportunity has parallels to the circumstellar habitable zone or *goldilocks zone* - the space around a star where the temperature is just right - not too hot and not too cold - for liquid water, and possibly life, to exist on a planet.

In contrast, the notion of *any* kind of unpredictability is anathema to many leaders. We strive to create well-oiled machines out of our organisations, which perform in a wholly predictable fashion. The machine converts resource and raw material into profit… and its job is done. These metaphorical machines are expressions of order, stability and structure. When fed correctly, they perform perfectly.

Actual machines such as internal combustion engines, steam turbines and electric motors are built from precision-engineered parts using the latest materials and conforming to very tight tolerances. They depend on high-quality, finely controlled fuel sources - putting diesel in your petrol-powered car (if you haven't already) should prove the point. Their environment is also critical. The power needs to be delivered in the right conditions for the result to be reliable and exploitable. Take your Ferrari off-road and you'll see what I mean.

The need for reliable components and a benign environment are two reasons why the machine metaphor for any organisation falls apart all too easily. This is why:

Any organisation can be characterised as one bunch of people doing stuff for another bunch of people. The architects of that stuff are people, and the beneficiaries are also people. Without people, somewhere in the system, there is no organisation - whether it is commercial, non-profit, government, military or academic. That remains an inviolable fact regardless of the degree of automation, artificial intelligence and technology, which is employed.

On that basis, it is people who form the primary cogs of the machine - and people, as you may have noticed, do not always perform in the most reliable, predictable and efficient manner. Human behaviour displays - to borrow a modern acronym - VUCA:

Volatility   Uncertainty   Complexity   Ambiguity

The environment in which the organisation operates has similar levels of unpredictability. It is the economy, and it generally manages to evade nearly all attempts to foresee what it will do next. If you don't believe me, try generating a reliable income from movements in foreign exchange rates. Prakash Loungani at the IMF analysed the accuracy of economic forecasters and found something both remarkable and worrying. "The record of failure to predict recessions is virtually unblemished," he said.

VUCA behaviour is not limited only to systems with many parts. Astronomy provides an example of how even very simple systems can behave in unpredictable ways: Take a solar system with a sun and a single planet. Knowing the positions, velocities and masses of the two bodies, their movements in space are simply described by equations which can be readily solved. Add a moon into the system and the equation can no longer be solved - the resulting 3-body system becomes 'chaotic' and requires different means of analysis, other than solving equations, to make approximations of its behaviour.

Dripping taps provide a much more accessible example of unpredictability in what appears to be a very simple system. As the tap is progressively turned, the flow reduces and the steady drip, drip, drip becomes unsteady and random in nature. We know it's going to drip, just never exactly when.

The digital processing power, which we have on hand today, allows us to simulate some of these complex behaviours accurately enough for us to have landed an interplanetary probe, 200 million km away, on the Churyumov–Gerasimenko comet measuring a just few kilometres across, in 2014.

Yet that same phenomenal computing power struggles to keep up with the weather. According to the European Centre for Medium-Range Weather Forecasts, the accuracy of 10-day predictions still fell below 50% in 2017. The UK Met Office's £97M Cray XC40 Supercomputer delivers very impressive short-term results of better than 98%. But if you want to know if it'll rain next week, you're better off tossing a coin.

Not only do the economy and the weather present us with forecasting challenges, they are also interdependent. We are all aware how a spell of good or bad weather can impact certain markets, but today there is growing evidence that the influence is bilateral - the economy is impacting the weather.

So, having hopefully established that both the economic environment in which organisations operate, and the human elements, which comprise them, are fundamentally volatile, uncertain, complex and ambiguous, the questions arise: So what? How do we change our leadership as a result?

The first change that we must make is to abandon all efforts to turn our organisations into well-oiled machines. Organisations striving for machine-like performance will not only fail to thrive but have difficulty surviving in an increasingly volatile world. Of course, this does not preclude integrating machine-like elements into our organisations: systems, production lines, structures, processes are the life-blood of organisational operations. But applying them to every aspect of activity is as harmful as removing all of them completely.

Chaos and stasis, although mutually exclusive, have one thing in common: They both deny life. Total chaos and absolute stasis are hostile to life, physically and psychologically. We need environments that provide us with the optimal degree of VUCA to thrive. We need to operate in that goldilocks zone of opportunity at neither one extreme, nor the other. Nature seems intrinsically to realise this, having made it (so far) impossible to achieve temperatures of absolute zero where entropy (a measure of chaos) becomes zero. At the other extreme it has managed to compensate most effectively for our attempts to ravage the planet, wreaking chaos through deforestation, nuclear fallout, oceanic pollution and all our other perturbations to the balance of the ecosystem we inhabit. Its extraordinary capacity for resilience is becoming increasingly compromised.

Our leadership of organisations needs to respect these simple facts of life. We do it by embracing the VUCA which we live in, not fighting it. It means we emulate our ecosystem rather than conflict with it. It also means that we integrate our humanity into our organisations rather than attempt to exclude it.

What does that look like?

At the strategic level it means focusing on the very highest good that we can deliver - individually and collectively - over and above the return, which it generates. More on this in a later chapter. If you hadn't noticed, this is exactly what our ecosystem does for us, constantly evolving in sophistication, creativity and variety - at least, when it's allowed to.

At the elemental level, it means acknowledging the VUCA of human nature - particularly the feeling side, explored in previous chapters. Remember how our seemingly alogical, irrational and unreasonable feelings determine the decisions we make.

Perhaps the most significant upshot of this view is seeing how utterly futile, damaging and desperate it is to apply machine-like strictures to the people who make our organisations - just as ruinous as leaving a vacuum of leadership in which chaos can reign.

Does this mean letting everyone run wild, doing what they want? No and Yes.

'Running wild' is just another form of chaos. We've all come across the Bull in the China Shop and the Loose Cannon - both unhelpful manifestations of disorder.

But *doing what you want* has some interesting ramifications. It is arguable that every human on the planet does what it wants anyway, at all times, given the situation it finds itself in. Is it conceivable, let alone possible, that any of us, at any time, have ever done what we didn't want to do? If every decision is made on a balance of feeling, we always do what we want - desire is a feeling. Even the act of sacrificing one's own good for another's can only come about if we prioritise the feeling of giving to the feeling of satisfying our own wellbeing. That is an act of free will, guided by feeling. Altruism is a mirage.

Even under duress and compulsion, we will pursue whatever action we associate with the least negative feeling.

This simple fact of human nature gives us, as leaders, a stark choice: Do we create rules that compel the behaviour we want from our people, or do we find people who resonate with our own vision of the organisation? Do we let people do what they want because it it coincides with what we want?

Let's apply *reductio ad absurdum* to both scenarios:

If we apply rules and regulations to the nth degree, it quickly reaches a point where the organisation seizes up completely - more time is spent on applying rules and checking for conformity than is spent on the operational mission. Does that sound familiar? Some organisations may well be guilty of this, but there's always further to go - we can tell people exactly what to say and do in every situation which arises. That already happens in some customer care call centres, which, incidentally, boast the highest staff turnover rates. Perhaps we could fit workers with an implant, which directs them at every decision-making point in their job, relieving them of any possibility of failure, inefficiency or mistake.

The 'absurd' alternative to the rule and regulation based organisation is to share your vision with your people, sit back and see what happens…

Clearly, the first scenario creates a living hell for anyone who wants to live *on purpose* and creates an environment hostile to physical and psychological wellbeing. Its scope is limited to that of the leader and no one else.

The success of the second scenario depends wholly on the resonance that can be achieved between your people and the organisation's raison d'être, or purpose. Its scope is unlimited.

Scenario 1 is machine-based, tending to order, structure, certainty and stasis

Scenario 2 is organic and seeks the edges of chaos, where life thrives.

Our leadership can only flourish if it respects life in its totality. Life comprises a delicate balance of rules and VUCA.

So if emulating machine behaviour dooms the organisation to failure, what metaphor could help us find that balance?

The answer is: the garden. The organisation as a garden and the leader as the gardener provides a healthy and sustainable metaphor on which to model our leadership behaviour. Here's why:

Gardeners' responsibilities are very well-defined. They concern themselves primarily with the environment, which boils down to the five elements: the quality of the earth; the quantity of water; adequate ventilation and protection from the wind (air); regulation of heat and light (fire); enough space for the plants to thrive (ether).

The gardener does not grow anything. The plants do the growing and don't need to be told how - they're really good at it - but they do need the right environment. An experienced gardener would never dig up a seed to find out how it's doing. They trust in the seed's innate intelligence, knowing that interference could harm its growth. Sometimes seeds don't germinate - that's fine, that's nature. Some plants need more water, some more support. The best gardens achieve a degree of diversity within limits set by the climate.

The garden metaphor is loaded with wisdom - how could you apply it to your organisation?

•

Roundup

- The edge of chaos exists somewhere between chaos and stasis - it's where the magic happens

- Certainty is death

- People are VUCA and so is the economy, so don't try and build a well-oiled machine

- "Do what you want" is a good place to start - as long as you are really clear on what you want

- The Garden is a good metaphor for organisations to reflect on

VALUES VS VALUE

What is aught, but as 'tis valued?

Lloyds Banking Group has three corporate values, one of which is: "Keeping it simple"

The Financial Times of 13 Jan 2019 wrote: "Lloyds Banking Group has been accused of 'gaming the system' by making its overdrafts more expensive and complicated…"

In addition to all the other well-publicised woes of this bank, it was allegedly using complexity as a competitive advantage, in direct violation of its own stated value.

Publishing corporate values sets most organisations up for a hiding to nothing. The values *will* be broken - sooner or later. Cynics will seek out examples of breached values - the impact of the public display of hypocrisy doing more harm than if the values had never been stated. Not difficult when you question what is achieved by broadcasting them in the first place.

Of course we can articulate values that are inviolable by making them sufficiently nebulous, as IKEA does with its value: "Striving to meet reality". Unfortunately this tactic renders the value as vacuous as it is bullet-proof.

All too often, values are the brain-children of board members - aided and abetted by consultants - who, rightly aspiring to the very highest standards, articulate values that are far removed from reality. The real values of any organisation are embedded in the behaviour of its members. The way a receptionist answers the phone will reveal far more about a business than any statement of values.

If you're worried about the values that your organisation embodies - a very valid concern - remember that your behaviour, as a leader, has more impact than any directive or statement. When you become aware of undesirable behaviour in the organisation, ask how it might be reflecting the behaviour of the leadership team. That doesn't always mean that you or your colleagues will be exhibiting the same behaviour, it often indicates that you are complicit in the errant behaviour by failing to challenge it effectively, and thus tacitly supporting it.

Personal values can also be of little worth and even somewhat counter-productive. Let's take three popular examples: integrity, loyalty, honesty.

The meaning of integrity as a value is not always clear. The true meaning is completeness or wholeness, but often advocates of integrity are referring to honesty which is quite a different concept. If we take it to mean being true to one's word, then the value precludes us from *ever* changing our minds - even in the rare event that doing so is for the greater good.

Loyalty, unlike trust, can be bought and frequently is. If you want to put it to the test, stop paying your employees to prove their loyalty to you and the organisation. Staying loyal to those who do not have your best interests at heart is, regrettably, an all too common occurrence; one to be avoided at all costs.

Honesty is undoubtedly the best policy in many circumstances - but not in all. Telling people exactly what you think of them, at every turn, is not a viable leadership strategy. Lying by omission is often preferable.

Notwithstanding the ease with which we can pick holes in many of the values that organisations hold as sacrosanct, and then go on to transgress, the real problem with them is that they are not absolute. They are all conditional on circumstance and relative to the individual. Discretion has to be applied and as soon as we do so, mine will be different from yours. I will be right and you will be wrong - vice versa from your point of view. In this way, values sow the seeds for conflict. Not only are they worthless, they are problematic.

Are there any absolute values that we can adopt? Perhaps the oracle's injunction to *Know Thyself* is as close as we can get.

Value, on the other hand, is central to the whole business of leading organisations, whose primary function is to manage the transaction of value. You do something for me - which I value - I give you something of value in return. Often the returned value is in the form of money - a promise of value to come. There is always a two-way exchange of value. Even in giving to a charity, the return value is the feeling of having done some good. That feeling is valuable to the giver - just as well since they get nothing else back. In fact, the value of anything is in the feeling it generates in the giver and receiver. The use of money as a signifier of value allows us to make transactions on a less emotional basis, but only because money has no inherent value, being at most a piece of paper, and at least a handful of electrons in a digital memory. Value evokes feeling - perhaps value *is* feeling?

So on that basis, the best way of receiving value, is to give value. The only way to pump-prime the process of giving and receiving - the transactional activity at the heart of our work - is to give value. We can't start it by taking - that is not going to make the other party feel good. But if we make them feel good by giving them what they want, they are more likely to give back. The same is true in terms of organisations and their markets.

The other very practical benefit of this approach is that we have total control over what we put out, none over what we get back. Putting our value out, because it feels good and right, regardless of the return, is the ultimate expression of authenticity - being true to yourself. All we need do is make sure that everything we do is what we *really* want - that it's on purpose.

Your value has nothing to do with your bank account, your house or your status. Your value is a combination of all your insights, your successes, your failures, your experiences, your thoughts and feelings, your relationships. Together they create huge potential to transform the world around you, through the people you lead. Similarly, your organisation's value is not in the balance sheet, the assets and the order book (though don't tell your FD). It lies in the potential of your people to deliver their collective value and make change.

This chapter's essential message is:

Put all your energies into delivering your value, and the rest will follow...

This applies not only to you, the leader, but everyone you lead - the entire organisation. For many organisations this means establishing a new balance between the focus on making money and delivering value. If your people have an innate belief that their purpose is to make money for the organisation, and that delivering value is a means to that end, there will be a fundamental dissonance, which will pervade the culture, promoting stress, conflict, disengagement, inefficiency and dissatisfaction. It's easy to see how this focus will undermine the very thing it is chasing.

I'm not suggesting for a moment that we leave finance to chance. Money needs discipline and regulation, but it is only ever a means to an end - never the end itself. When it usurps purpose, trouble ensues.

Conversely, when organisations prioritise the delivery of their value over any return, the culture resonates with our innate human nature and desires, creating fulfilment, impact, abundance, exhilaration, meaning, freedom and fun.

•

Roundup

- Values are not worth the wall they're posted on

- Behaviours eat values for breakfast

- One value worth any salt is: Know Thyself

- Value is tangible - you can *feel* it. You can't feel money or profit

- Focus on the Value you and your organisation delivers - what you get back needs far less attention

UPSIDE DOWN LEADERSHIP

Up and down, up and down, I will lead them up and down

Some received wisdom on organisational leadership is not only ignorant of reality, but damaging to boot. Many of these erroneous concepts have been touched upon in earlier chapters. Here is a summary of what not only needs changing in our leadership thinking, but in some cases reversing 180°:

Slow Down Your Judgement

The faculty of judgement discriminates situations and people into good and bad. In reality they are neither. Good and bad are human constructs. Judgement is a powerful weapon, which we need to wield with care. Of course you can't sit on the fence for ever, but make sure you take in the view on both sides, before you get off.

Understand Your Stress

Stress is a human artefact, which has no basis in the situation you associate with it, only with the person experiencing it. Changing anything external to alleviate it is always and only a short-term solution. Examine your internal dynamics and understand that this is where the permanent resolution lies.

Feel Deeply

Every decision you make is based on how you feel, not what you think. Never dismiss how you feel - embrace it. Sensitise yourself to how you feel. Remember that only feelings will tell you when something is out of balance and needs adjustment. If you don't respond to those feelings, they will grow until you do. Don't wait for physical symptoms to make changes - it may be too late.

Balance Work With Rest

The quality of your work will only be as good as that of your rest. Schedule the highest quality rest into your day, every day. Rest is not zoning out, having a chat or browsing LinkedIn. The best rest is doing nothing whilst fully conscious and aware. True mindfulness will help you rest whilst meditation will create the right foundation.

Live On Purpose

Know your purpose and align your work to it. Until you have a clarity of purpose which resonates with your innermost being, work will lack fulfilment and satisfaction, no matter how successful you are, and how much you achieve. Remember that purpose is what you put out, not what you get back.

Take Responsibility

Ultimately, you are responsible for what you think and feel. You may have little control over the situation you find yourself in, but you have total control over how you respond to it. If you let your reactive habits control your behaviour, you throw away your power to change your experience.

Forgive, Never Forget

To blame someone is to deny your own power. Forgiveness is to reclaim that power and to let go of *your* burden - nothing to do with anyone else. You do not have the power to absolve others of their mistakes - so don't bother trying - only they can do that. Always remember, as forgetting is also a loss of power.

Delegate Trust

To delegate means to unleash or unbind. Many leaders delegate activity but retain responsibility (the ability to respond) because they lack trust. Delegating trust is a prime directive of leadership without which people and organisations cannot grow, evolve and thrive.

Garden Your Organisation

Most organisational metaphors - military, sports, machine - are win/lose. The organisation-as-garden metaphor is win/win because it respects the fundamental nature of both its environment and its constituents as being intrinsically unpredictable, uncertain, organic and alive.

Coach Your People

Telling people what to do may be needed on occasion but in reality, they need to be telling you what to do. Your leadership supports their work, not the other way around. Coaching them gets them to look inwards to their own self-leadership - the fastest route for their evolution and development.

Be Your Own Hero

Stop using other people as your frame of reference. Use your self. The sooner you acknowledge that you are unique in your situation, experience, purpose and aspiration, the sooner you'll realise that no one but you is better placed to lead yourself. Read widely and listen to others but never emulate them in pursuit of their success.

Don't Should Or Shouldn't

Doing what you should may serve you well at times. But doing it all the time means you'll be doing what you don't *want* much of the time. This creates an instant misalignment - a discordance - between your purpose and your action, a sure recipe for unhappiness and failure to achieve your desires.

Serve Your People

Service is always from the more developed, to the less developed. You only appreciate service when it's done for you better than you could do it yourself. Service is not servile, it is a prime directive of leadership, providing an environment for others to prosper.

Deliver Your Value

Whatever your innate value is, and that of your organisation or team, prioritise giving it over all else. Of course maintain all the good practices, which running a business demands, but use them as a means to the ultimate end of being valuable.

Express Gratitude

Not just saying thank you. This is about actively looking for others' good work and decision-making, and letting them know you appreciate it. It lifts you and them - and makes it much easier to address deficiencies and mistakes when they occur, not just at the annual appraisal. Done well, it can render appraisals not just redundant, but undesirable.

Measure With Care

Measuring lead times, failure rates, staff turnover and share price are just a few of the variables, which can be measured accurately. In each case there is a fixed unit of measurement, which can be used to compare performance between organisations. Employee engagement, commitment, trust, loyalty and talent cannot be measured rigorously - beware of trying to do so.

Play The Infinite Game

Don't play to win or lose - play to stay in the game. The game of leadership has no end - it's an infinite game. Don't model your organisation on sports or military metaphors - they are finite games. Remember that the purpose of life is to live - not to get to the end. You're not going to be taking that much with you so enjoy the time you have.

Define Your Medium-Level Abstraction (MLA)

Articulate your mission with just the right amount of definition to inspire others with the prospect of delivering all their energy, ability and value to the enterprise. The goldilocks zone for leadership lies somewhere between the chaos of ambiguity and the stasis of micromanagement.

Try Doing Less

The world of work is an abundant one. However much we do, we never finish it - there is always more. Doing more and more is not sustainable. Operating at 100% capacity day in and day out is neither healthy nor balanced. Try doing less to see what happens. How do you get to go home at 5.30 pm everyday? You go home at 5.30 pm everyday.

Look Inwards Often

Our attention is largely consumed by the world our five senses bring to us. Our inner world of being, thinking and feeling deserves at least as much attention, engagement and curiosity. Turn your attention through 180° frequently.

You're Already There

All the thoughts you've thought, the feelings you've had, the things you've said and the decisions you've made have all come together to create your experience right here, right now. There's nowhere to go - you're already there.

•

Roundup

- Forgive all, forget nothing

- Balance work with rest

- Delegate activity, responsibility and trust

- Feel grateful and express it

- Prioritise delivering value

THE BROKEN CEO

CONCLUSION

The purpose of this book is to remind us that our experience of life and leadership is as much to do with our inner dynamics as our outer circumstances. Yogic wisdom, and many other sources of metaphysical knowledge, would have it that our entire lives are created by thought, and thought alone. This book is not attempting to convince you of that, or indeed anything, other than the wisdom of your own experience - which is all we really have to go on in the final analysis.

Knowing yourself - self-awareness - is the objective. The means and the end are one: attention. For that reason alone, should some or all of the contents of this book prove intellectually indigestible to you, I would refer you to the appendix on meditation. If you do nothing else, meditation will put you on a path (your path) towards knowing more about yourself.

One of the benefits of seeing, first-hand, how we have made ourselves susceptible to habit in the form of negative, reactive behaviours, is that we begin to realise how, far from operating solely in us, they must also be playing a greater or lesser part in how others present themselves to the world. In others words, it becomes far more difficult to judge and condemn others' behaviours, when we see the exact same dynamics operating within ourselves. How close does any judgement of another bring us to a charge of hypocrisy?

At first this inner awareness puts us in conflict with many of our treasured opinions, mindsets and beliefs - just like Arjuna and his loved ones in the opposing army. Challenging them can be an uncomfortable business at times. Yet the indisputable centre of calm, serene clarity, which is available to connect with, reduces the resistance to insignificance - providing we persist.

The benefits to our leadership are immense:

- Our decision-making improves
- Our relationships become deeper
- Our mental health benefits
- Our energy increases
- Our stress reduces
- Our purpose becomes clearer
- Our behaviour becomes more compassionate

Inevitably these changes, however incremental, impact on others both consciously and subconsciously. This is the basis of culture change which can never be sustainable as a project or initiative. Behaviour is contagious - particularly that from a superior - and spreads more powerfully through embodying it than any other form of communication.

On that basis alone, culture comes from the top - from the CEO. Those who resonate with it amplify it. Those who don't eventually leave for a culture that suits them.

In conclusion, the nugget of knowledge I would have you take away from this book is that of self-referencing - being true to yourself above all else - however challenging that may seem at times. Or in the words of Ralph Waldo Emerson:

To be yourself in a world that is constantly trying to make you something else is the greatest accomplishment.

APPENDICES

APPENDIX 1 - MEDITATION

Meditation is a widely misunderstood practice. Strictly speaking, it's not even a practice, more a state of mind. Perhaps the reason meditation is so misunderstood is that we try to understand it intellectually when it operates outside our intellects. What that means is there is no point thinking about it. Thinking about meditation is not meditating! The good part of that is that you can't fail at at it - you either do it… or you don't.

Like many things, the proof is in the pudding. Does meditating change you, your relationships, your life? My answer to that is an unequivocal *yes!* My experience, and that of my clients, to whom I introduce it, is that meditation makes for a calmer, clearer existence, in which stress has less impact, relationships become more harmonious and the ups and downs of the world around us affect us less. The desperation to achieve abates and we enjoy inactivity as much as activity.

But my experience is mine, not yours. So instead of concerning yourself with how it works, if it will work or why it works, I suggest you try it. 3rd party proof, statistics and scientific studies on the effects of meditation are just intellectual noise, which can easily delay your own experience.

So this is how you start:

Time of Day

The best time is first thing in the morning, before breakfast - ideally before sunrise, though that can be challenging in some latitudes. Children can also make this time impractical. If you can't meditate in the morning, the evening works well too. You may have to experiment to find your best time. Meditating during the day can be problematic, not just from a practical point of view, but energetically - we are not as well disposed to sitting still. However meditating at any time is preferable to not meditating at all.

Duration

Some first-time meditators have difficulty with more than a couple of minutes. Others settle into 10 or 20 minutes without a problem. The important thing is to go with whatever works for you. Daily practice is the initial goal - practising everyday or as frequently as possible. Better to meditate for two minutes everyday for a week, than 30 minutes on a Sunday. See how long is comfortable and establish it as a daily practice for a month. Then start to gently increment it up to 20 minutes a day. Use a gentle alarm so you don't have to check the time.

Things to avoid

Don't practice after eating, or drinking alcohol. If you're feeling very emotional or very tired, skip the practice - there's always tomorrow. If you are undergoing any mental health treatment, check with your therapist or doctor before you start meditating. Finally, if you experience any significant levels of anxiety during meditation, stop and come back to it another time.

Environment

Quiet surroundings are generally helpful to establishing a meditation practice, but if you can't find quiet, don't let that stop you. Try to use the same place every day if you can - this is part of creating a helpful habit to support the practice against the many reasons we can all find for not doing it. Use an upright chair - the kind you might have at a dinner table, or in your kitchen.

Posture

Sit with your spine straight, away from the back of the chair and your feet flat on the floor. Keep your head level, neither up nor down. Put your hands on your legs or in your lap. Close your eyes.

Practice

Focus your attention on your breath going in and out of your nose. If your nose is blocked, breathe through your mouth! Be aware of the air flowing in and out of you. If you are breathing through your nose, let the attention settle at the bridge, between the eyes and feel the breath flowing there. That's all you do: be aware of the breath flowing in and out.

Distractions

Sooner or later a thought will intrude: "Am I doing this right? Is it working? What am I meant to be feeling? Where is the transcendental experience? What shall I have for lunch? I need to scratch an itch. How long do I have left? What time is it? I need to look at my bank balance when I've finished. I wonder if my mother will phone tonight" etc. etc. etc. There is no end to the thinking.

You will not stop the thinking - don't even try. Just come back to the point of attention. By trying to stop the thinking, you will just create more. The mind is meant to think, just like the heart is meant to pump. You will find that as you maintain focus on the breath, both your heart and your thinking will slow, but without any help from you!

Whether you find that your meditation is very chaotic - full of thoughts, feelings and distractions - or very serene, calm and peaceful, it doesn't matter. That may sound strange but remember that our intellects are dead set on making everything good or bad. In truth meditation is neither. It cannot fail. The only failure is not practising. Also remember that it is operating *under the radar* - subconsciously - so don't judge it.

Afterwards

It is very common to feel a sense of tranquillity, ease and well-being after meditating - though as I said above, it doesn't matter if you don't. When you do, keep it with you and don't let it dissipate too easily. Maintaining that sense of presence and serenity is the basis of mindfulness, another good practice to explore and establish. Though be mindful that much of what has been written about mindfulness is commercially motivated and not always accurate.

Pause regularly during the day and immerse yourself in that feeling of peace for a few seconds.

Long term

Once you've established a practice, you'll probably be drawn to learning more about meditation. Beware that meditation is a long-term business - it's a lifetime practice - so the real authorities on meditation will have experience measured in decades, not months or even years. Meditation has religious and spiritual connotations which put many people off taking it up. The truth is that meditation is not a religious practice, although many religions promote meditation or practices, which appear similar. Meditation does not require any belief other than in your own existence and experience. In this respect, atheists and devout believers are very similar - they both believe in something, which is not necessarily known and experienced: the believer in a deity; the atheist in the impossibility of a deity. The agnostic, on the other hand, admits to not knowing.

Whatever your belief-system, investigate what you are drawn to, being aware of the resonance it has with your deepest being. Only you will know which path to follow. Moderation is a good thing - try what you are drawn to but don't flit from one thing to another like a butterfly - give each experiment time, or stick with what works for you.

Resources

The style of meditation that suits you may well be different from mine - it's a very personal choice. Here are a few resources, which may be of value to you:

The *Transcendental Meditation* technique or TM is a form of silent mantra meditation, developed by Maharishi Mahesh Yogi.

The *School of Meditation* is 57 years old and has taught meditation to thousands of people. It's a non-profit, registered charity based in London but also has branches around the UK

The *London Buddhist Centre* teaches meditation and Buddhism in a way that is relevant to modern London life. It is a public centre, open to all, with no expectation of Buddhist involvement.

APPENDIX 2 - PROGRAMMES

You'll find some of the changes to your leadership, which are detailed in this book, straightforward. Sometimes we're so ready for change, just a small nudge will make it happen. I have experienced many times over how the best advice comes as confirmation of what we already know, but may not have actioned.

Other behavioural shifts need a little more time, energy and persistence. The programmes outlined below provide a blend of weekly, online material, supported by regular 1-on-1 meetings, to support sustainable change. The material covers much of the contents of this book, and more. The meetings provide an opportunity to explore how the material relates specifically to you and your live work challenges. The combination is a powerful catalyst for transformation.

LEAD Programme

The Leadership Evolution and Accelerated Development programme comprises 3 modules corresponding to parts 2,3 and 4 of this book:

- Personal Evolution - explores your mental and emotional dynamics and their impact on your life

- Relationship Evolution - applies the personal insights to your relationships with others

- Leadership Evolution - embeds the personal and relationship shifts into your leadership of others.

The programme delivers 24 weeks of material supported by nine 1-on-1 meetings.

Personal Evolution Programme

This equates to the first module of the LEAD programme, which focuses on your inner, mental and emotional dynamics and unfolds over 8 weeks with 4 x 1-on-1 meetings.

Management Evolution Programme

A bespoke, 8 week programme designed specifically for your needs and challenges as a senior manager, comprising weekly, online material and 4 x 1-on-1 meetings.

Bootstrap Programme

A 3 week programme comprising material and 2 x 1-on-1 meetings, laser-focused on your challenge.

•

Client feedback

"I would absolutely recommend the LEAD Programme for the experienced professional who needs to take time to reflect and push on to the next level." Nick F - HRD

"The following 6 months changed not only my methods at work but some of the driving thoughts deep within too. The bonus being how much it helped me beyond work, at home and personally." Chris L - FD

"I now feel much more in control of my life, worry a lot less and can properly switch off, which I struggled with massively before." - Graeme H - CEO

For more information email: lead@chrispearse.co.uk

APPENDIX 3 - RESOURCES

Here are some of my online resources which provide more perspective on the very broad subject of leadership:

    linkedin.com/in/chrispearse1/

    forbes.com/sites/chrispearse/

    chrispearse.co.uk/

The books listed below have been important influences on the writing of this book:

    Emotional Intelligence - Daniel Goleman

    Navigating Complexity - Arthur Battram

    Autobiography of a Yogi - Paramahamsa Yogananda

    The Republic - Plato

    Inner Engineering - Sadhguru

    Tao Te Ching - Lao Tsu

ABOUT THE AUTHOR

I initially discovered my outer purpose at around 8 years old, when I developed an insatiable appetite for taking things apart. Anything from alarm clocks and radios to bicycles and lawnmowers. My parents often provided the right incentive for putting them back together again, affording even more learning.

Engineering was on the cards as a career, until I fell in love with chemistry, building a makeshift laboratory in the garage. I was besotted with the appearance of different chemicals, their smell, the way they reacted together and the colours they gave to flames. I loved the glassware, the retorts, beakers and test tubes. Chemistry became my new fixation… until I blew myself up in a silly experiment. I should have known better.

On completing a degree in electrical and electronic engineering, I threw myself into designing the hardware and software to control a variety of applications from networking computers, to digital effects for film and TV.

About The Author

At around 30 I began to feel a different calling - one that involved technology *and* people. Within a year I found myself working abroad having set up a new business, selling and marketing technology across southern Europe. A number of commercial roles followed culminating in a leadership role with a global remit.

Looking back on this period I see clearly that it was instrumental in teaching me how organisations and the people within them worked. The same curiosity I had as an 8 year old was alive and well. But the real game changer for me was understanding that our behaviour as human beings follows a completely different set of rules from that of the mechanical, chemical and electronic systems I loved.

I studied personal development, psychology, metaphysics, yoga, organisational development, coaching and leadership, meeting many remarkable minds en route. I balanced my learning of the outer world with insights into my inner world through reflection, contemplation and meditation. Far from being incompatible, as I had feared, they quickly became integrated - I could no longer make sense of the world of people and organisations without reference to my own inner world. The hermetic expression, As Above, So Below, showed the way.

Soon I was working with leaders, directors and senior managers of many different shapes and sizes of organisation - multinationals, bluechips, government, universities, charities, and small businesses. I found the same dynamics at play in all of them. All of them subject to many of the symptoms and causes explored in this book. All of them potentially able to change for the better through looking inward, as well as outward.

Today, a feeling of awe at the world we inhabit, and our own existence, swamps any pride in what I've learnt - the more I learn, the more I realise how little I know.

ALSO...

If you liked this book, please take the time to review it on Amazon.

Send a link or a screenshot of a review that you've written about this book to:

review@chrispearse.co.uk

and you will receive access to the High-Impact Leadership Scorecard, to score yourself across several aspects of leadership and identify opportunities for further development. On completion you'll also be eligible for an Audible coupon enabling you to download the audio version of this book free of charge.

Thank you for reading The Broken CEO - I hope it has given you value and inspired you to be the leader you always wanted to be.

Printed in Great Britain
by Amazon